AF539286

VIENNA

Hans Weigel
Ernst Hausner

VIENNA

Hans Weigel
Ernst Hausner

Jugend und Volk
Wien München

ISBN 3 - 7141 - 6056 - 6
Jugend und Volk Wien
ISBN 3 - 8113 - 6056 - 6
Jugend und Volk München
2nd edition 1977

4184 - 77/2/30

Design: Ernst Hausner-Stollhofen
English Translation: Renate Welsh
French Translation: Michèle Rössner
Italian Translation: Livia Tonelli
Printed by Tusch-Druck GmbH, Vienna

Hans Weigel

VIENNA IS DIFFERENT

VIENNA IS DIFFERENT

Everything is different here. Nothing is what it seems, what its name would imply, what you would expect.

First of all, the city of Vienna does not lie on the Danube. It lies on a river by the name of Wien which is not really a river, and actually Vienna does not lie on it either. As soon as it (the river) approaches the town in a delicate trickle it is hidden and vaulted over.

Only in the last leg of its course does the Wien play the proper role of a river with a city lying on it: it surfaces and flows in full sight, pleasantly incorporated into the cityscape, towards its mouth which it reaches all too soon. It graces the Stadtpark, it separates the Ministry of War (which no longer is one) from the Wholesale Market Hall (which is called that despite the fact that it no longer bears that name) and flows past the Main Customs Office (which is also called that despite the fact that it no longer bears that name), and there is its mouth already, but by no means in the Danube but in the Danube Canal on whose banks Vienna also lies and which is no Canal but rather an arm of the Danube.

The bed of the Wien is huge, deep and broad, elaborately designed and almost completely dry. If one looks very closely — and only then — one discovers a rather ridiculous trickle down there. This river dwarf in the gigantic river bed has the effect of a baby in a great four-poster bed. One almost gets the impression that this disparity must be due to megalomania, that the great city tried to upgrade the river which shares its name. One could not be more wrong. The little Wien, outwardly harmless and innocuous, frequently used to become dangerous over night. For centuries it overflowed its banks in spring and caused great damage until the great mayor Dr. Karl Lueger insisted on its regulation. Approaching the city from the West one sees the generous construction and the little rivulet before it runs its subterranean course, harmless, idyllic and yet demonic and dangerous by nature — a symbol, a landmark, a leitmotiv.

The assertation of this Viennese duality — harmless-demonic — is by no means new, but neither is it as old as one might believe. For a long time, for all too long a time, Vienna cherished her role as a capital of joie de vivre, of optimism and easy-going indolence, as attested among others by Goethe and Schiller ("Sunday forever, forever turning the spit on the hearth") and Grillparzer ("Enervating is thy summer breeze, thou Capua of the spirit"). Vienna did not protest against the motto "life's a dance" which was claimed for Viennese music, against dancing and dance music being understood as a self-portrayal rather than a way out, as diagnosis rather than therapy. Well into the period of operetta and the pioneer years of the sound film industry Vienna was presented as lively and jolly. Only the dual catastrophe of apocalyptic dimensions with its dual special visitation of the city brought to the surface the question of whether the native dance in three-four time had not been a dance on a vulcano.

Only in the decades since it arose from the ashes of the Second World War has Vienna tried to see its own image anew, discovered the demonic behind the harmless façade and retroactively as it were rebuilt its own past. Since then one keeps hearing from thoughtful and intelligent Viennese that Vienna has nothing to do with its cliché. In fact the negation of the cliché has become so prevalent that it is in danger of turning into a cliché in its own right.

This may have something to do with the fact that the city of Vienna entered a new, most surprising and highly challenging phase of its existence in 1955 with the signing of the State Treaty and the restitution of Austrian sovereignty. Tracing the emotional responses of Vienna into the past one keeps stumbling upon a recently past "good old time" and an evil present.

After the dissolution of the Holy Roman Empire in the Napoleonic era absolutism overshadowed the *Biedermeier* — then the brief period of stability after the Congress of Vienna was the "good old times". The chaos and libertinism of the violent explosion of the revolution of 1848 frightened both conservatives and liberals and after the bloody liquidation of the revolution the darkest reaction triumphed — and the *Biedermeier* period became the "good old times". At the beginning of the 'seventies of the last century the "Black Friday" of the stock-market crash brought tremendous social and economic unrest, and the preceding *Gründerjahre,* years of unfettered industrial expansion and speculation, however hectic and lacking in solidity they had been, became the "good old times". Round the turn of the century the disintegration and agony of the Danube Monarchy became more and more clearly apparent, the façade of prosperity was gradually undermined by national and political tensions and catastrophies. Even before the outbreak of the First World War Karl Kraus had spoken of the "Austrian testing ground for the end of the world". Despite that many backward-looking optimists viewed that "world of yesterday" as the "good old times" in retrospect. After the war which was started in Vienna and was to become the First World War the end-of-the-world mentality was as it were permanently established in Vienna, even though much suggested "good new times" just then: municipal housing, schools, and health service. In *"La Valse"* Maurice Ravel sketched a portrait of the city which tried in vain to establish the link with its "classical" waltz past.

In the face of continuing crises and of permanent deterioration an upgrading of the past and the establishment of the cliché were necessary acts of self-defence. Representative for many observers, the surgeon Theodor Billroth, Viennese by choice, could say at that time: "Everything is *gemütlich* here . . . here we sing and make music and go to the theatre and go to hear Strauss and with him dig our heads into the sand of our *gemütlichkeit.*" The two time-honoured local formulas "Something's got to happen" and "There's nothing to be done about it" had become identical, fatalism and flight from reality had become a meaningful way of life. Thus Vienna became a city of the arts, in particular of the theatre. But after the consolidation through the currency reform (1948) and the departure of the occupying forces (1955) there was an unexpected change of fortune. The city which in living memory had always floated from crisis to crisis, from bankruptcy to bankruptcy, from catastrophe to catastrophe, whose hymns had kept changing — from Haydn's *Kaiserlied* via a short-lived unpopular republican hymn back to the Haydn melody, first with a text praising the native soil and then proclaiming *Deutschland über alles* had always given priority to the inofficial Viennese hymns: from the legendary folk singer Augustin with his merry "Everything's gone" and the related song from Nestroy's "Lumpazivagabundus" presenting the apocalyptic "The world will certainly not last much longer" in happy three-four time and ending in a *Jodler,* to the resigned "Fledermaus" statement, again in three--four time, "Happy he who forgets what cannot be changed". Now this city oriented on destruction was suddenly and quite unpreparedly faced with the blessings of peace, prosperity, economic growth and political stability.

A new crisis grew up, a crisis which consisted of there not being a crisis. Fatalism was redundant. Flight from reality was a luxury. For the first time Vienna could afford to confront its present without justified fear of the future. Vienna found time and strength to catch her breath in a situation which in a total European context could be termed *gemütlich,* and to realize: We are not *gemütlich* at all! Vienna lived her present, looked at herself and mustered her past, and a clever man said at the beginning of the 'sixties: "The good old times are now!"

But an attitude rooted in the soul as well as in tradition cannot be changed radically over night. Irrealities and contradictions are too deeply imbedded in the face of the city to be mellowed, let alone dissolved, within a short time. Vienna had lived in a permanently revokable relationship with the world of realities, under the mottoes of "Despite" and "As if". But just as she had mastered times of trouble, she eventually mastered prosperity, too. Distress had not broken Vienna, and neither did the fat years (there were two times seven, approximately).

In the meantime the last "good old time" to date has retired into the past. We realize with relief that we have come through unscathed. We have serious worries again, we are once again "happily unhappy, just like some people are unhappily happy" (Ferdinand Raimund).

Just as the city of Vienna does not lie on the Danube, despite general claims to this fact (one might rather say: the Danube lies on the city of Vienna), as this Danube is greenish or brownish and by no means blue, as the *Theater an der Wien* does not lie on the Wien, as a square in Vienna is called *"Schottentor"* despite the fact that there has not been a gate there for over a hundred years, so contradictions abound elsewhere in the image of the city.

The Ringstrasse, popularly known as "the Ring", is of course no ring but rather a semi- or three-quarter circle, an arc with the Franz-Josephs-Kai along the banks of the Danube Canal forming the chord.

This Ring, which celebrated its one hundredth anniversary some time back, surrounds the "Inner City", the first of the twenty-three districts, which, even though it is merely one twenty-third of the city, is generally called "the city". The Viennese say "I am going into the city" when they mean going to the centre from within the city.

Before approaching the question of whether the Ring is indeed, as is often claimed, one of the most beautiful streets in the world, one has to ask oneself what constitutes the beauty of a city or a street. On this occasion one can sketch a sort of Theory of Relativity for form in art and landscape.

I know that the Matterhorn in Switzerland, the Hohe Munde in the Tyrol, Rax and Schneeberg to the South of Vienna and the Leopoldsberg just outside Vienna have not changed externally over the last few centuries, and yet they look different now than at the beginning of the age of Alpinism. I know that the State Opera, the Musikverein building, the Post Office Savings Bank have not changed in the last decades, and yet they look different now than they did under Franz Josef I. A view does not only depend on the image but also on the viewer and his time. Even films change over the years. And in the same way the Ring has also been subjugated to the relativity principle.

A building, totally identical with itself, looks different when horse-drawn carriages drive past it than when electric trams go past. It looks different when I see it every day than when I saw it years ago and dreamed about it for years and then see it again. The Vienna State Opera looked different when Gustav Mahler, Franz Schalk or Karl Böhm was its director.

The Ring was always a beautiful boulevard as regards the sidewalks, the roads, the trees and the parks. It was created when Emperor Franz Josef had the old fortifications razed. The inner city, freed from its fetters, spilled out in all directions when at last the city was no longer identical with the "city" but former suburbs and surrounding villages were incorporated and it could extend continuously to the Danube and to the slopes of the Vienna Woods (which are no woods but a range of hills).

On both sides of the boulevard large, highly ornate buildings of representational character went up: Burgtheater, Opera, museums, the Stock Exchange, Parliament, the Town Hall, the University — all in the elaborate eclectic style of the *Gründerzeit,* pseudo Gothic, fake Renaissance, antiquity in the style of wedding-cake decoration. In the upsurge of the time of its creation this "Ringstrassen style" may have had a kind of beauty of its own. When *Jugendstil* and *Secession* had ushered in a new architectural era, the style become more and more unbearable. Meanwhile, however, history has coloured our view. The Vienna Town Hall always seemed ugly to me in its pretence of original Gothic. When I saw the building again in the autumn of 1945, after more than seven years of absence, the building had acquired so much political substance that I now see it with different eyes. It has become more of the essence of a city than an expression of architectural taste at sea. Thus all the Ringstrassen buildings have changed, they become different when we envisage a century as we look at them.

And thus the general question of the beauty of a city arises. Perfect beauty does not exist. Not even Salzburg is beautiful on all points. I believe that a "beautiful city" has a mysterious power of integrating even that which is not beautiful.

Without doubt the Ring's generosity, its spatiousness was and is great and almost unique. It is Imperial in its scope. It realizes a great design in sovereign creative lavishness which only absolutism could afford.

There is for instance a square flanked by two large museums with fat Empress Maria Theresia enthroned on a hybrid monument in the middle. At the back there is the genuine and noble façade of the former court stables, virtually free from any disfiguration, now the Trade Fair Palace, juxtaposed beyond the Ring by the Outer Burg Gateway forming the fourth side and there is so much width, so much measure, this is so much an Imperial city in the best sense that the eclectic cupolas and the over-monumental Maria Theresia become insignificant.

Many Viennese squares share that characteristic, they are not closed in by façades on four sides but rather reach beyond themselves, suggesting wide open spaces.

Beyond the Outer Burg Gate stretches the prime example of that species, the *Heldenplatz,* framed on three sides by distant silhouettes rather than façades, totally unlike a square in the sense of an open-air hall but rather a wide space. Here again architectural quality is ennobled by the setting. While the Danube is not blue, the centre of Vienna is very green, especially here where the *Volksgarten,* the Burggarten and the park of the Town Hall follow one upon the other, linked by the trees lining the Ring, where generous space discloses the great secret of a beautiful city and where from one blessed point in front of the *Hofburg* the silhouette of the hills of the Vienna Woods presents itself.

The wedding-cake Gothic of the Votive Church, a little further down the Ring by the *Schottentor* lies spendidly in an open space that any genuine cathedral might envy. If the *Votivkirche* was one, the beauty of it would be unbearably painful.

St. Stephen's on the other hand, in the centre of the centre, is a genuine and great Gothic cathedral. For that reason its position has to be so disadvantageous. There is no point from which it can be seen in its entirety, only the high spire with its incomprehensibly harmonious synthesis of massiveness and slenderness can be seen from many sides.

And the other Gothic jewel of the inner city, St. Mary's on the Banks (needless to say it does not lie on any banks whatsoever), is so helplessly shoved into narrow twisting lanes that it is hard to find and even harder to get a proper view of it.

The beauties of the beautiful inner city are mostly secretive beauties which do not offer themselves but need to be discovered and tracked down: courtyards, hallways, unknown corners, little lanes, small squares, façades hidden in narrow mazes, small churches with unpromising exteriors and grandiose interiors.

One square only proves the rule as the great exception: the Baroque *Josefsplatz* (of the open-air hall type) with the façade of the National Library, a part of the *Hofburg* which is no *burg* but rather a town by itself, a town within a town within a town, a compendium of Viennese architectural history and an Austrian symbol to boot, preaching the grace of the unfinished: the large newest wing of the Hofburg (from which Adolf Hitler proclaimed his "mission accomplished") planned as the official residence, was finished too late to be occupied by the Hapsburgs. It is also built in the *Ringstrassen* style and only the first half of a gigantic project which would have disfigured the *Heldenplatz* and thus the face of Vienna. The Hapsburgs were overthrown in time.

Opposite the Inner Burg Gate, on *Michaelerplatz,* the great Viennese architect Adolf Loos provocatively built his house without ornament to annoy the emperor — and not only him. When *art nouveau* was fashionable and modern art *Secessionist* in style, he radically overtook his generation. He was a great and unrecognized son of his city, a passionate negator. Two volumes of his writings he called "Despite" and "Spoken into Emptiness". He was the prototype of the uncomfortable Viennese, one of the prophets, whose time can only commence under the sign of the anti-cliché. He rediscovered that genuine pure beauty which had vanished and been betrayed since the end of the Baroque period — needless to say that to her shame Vienna let him build only a very few houses.

The great axis of the Inner City is called *Kärntnerstrasse* from the Ring to St. Stephen's and from there to the *Franz-Josefs-Kai Rotenturmstrasse*. It runs approximately North-South. There is no corresponding East-West axis, so as to make sure that no pedantic clarity might take over, so that the highlights have every chance to hide, among them many important town palaces, usually with exotic names and of aristocratic hue: Palffy, Pallavicini, Wilczek, Lobkowitz, Kinsky, Esterhazy . . . all bearing witness to Vienna's past as an Imperial capital and residence.

Of the many Viennese railway-stations two have been generously renovated, and it is no accident that these two are the Western and Southern stations.

As in the past, one goes West to Switzerland, to France, to the Federal Republic of Germany, to Holland and Belgium. As in the past one goes South to Italy and Yugoslavia.

The compass, however, has four points, and the Viennese compass had even more than four, since the important Viennese railway stations were the Western, Southern, Eastern, Northern, Northwestern and the Franz Josef's Station.

Accordingly one might say the Viennese points of the compass were called West, South, East, North and Franz Josef. This fifth direction is no longer in demand. One used to take the *Franz-Josefs-Bahn* to Prague, Dresden, Berlin — now one goes from Vienna to Gmünd. From the Eastern Station (which has now been joined to the Southern Station) one used to depart to Budapest, now it tends to be Bruck an der Leitha. The Northern and North-Western Stations no longer exist, any more than the electric tramline to Bratislava known as the *"Preßburger Elektrische"*. To the North and to the East Vienna is separated from her past by a close and more or less tight Iron Curtain. In 1948 this capped a development which had begun thirty years earlier. One morning in 1918 seven million Austrians woke up to find that their grandparents had become foreigners.

The motto "Vienna will always be Vienna", half promise, half threat, has proved itself true and almost prophetic in every way. Vienna has always been Vienna. From early *Babenberger* days round the turn of the first millenium Vienna had been a "capital city", but the organism whose head remained and lasted varied from the beginning. Vienna always was more of a capital *per se* than capital of any particular state or Empire.

It was the residence of the Emperors of the Holy Roman Empire which was neither holy nor Roman and not really quite definable in terms of constitutional law. The treasury in the *Hofburg* preserves the crown and other Imperial jewels and insignia, the vault below the Church of the Capuchins shows visitors an imposing range of most illustrious sarcophagi.

When in the face of the Napoleonic challenge Emperor Franz liquidated the Holy Roman Empire and thereby at the very last moment formalized an established fact, he called himself by his official Imperial title in the official patent which effected that dissolution. Thus the Roman Emperor Franz II, King "in Germania, Hungaria, Bohemia" etc. and "ever augmentor of the Realm" put his seal to the diminuation of that realm. The new Emperor after Emperor Franz was Emperor Franz, and while he started his career as Emperor Franz II he ended it as Emperor Franz I. Only now the Hapsburgs were "Emperors of Austria", but at the same time Kings of Hungary, of Bohemia, of Croatia, Slavonia, Lodomeria, Grand Dukes of Toscana and Cracow, Dukes of Friaul, Modena, Parma, Piacenza and Guastalla, Kings of Jerusalem and much else besides. The official Imperial title in its full verbiage was very much an evening's programme to the very end in 1918 and a weird mixture of reality and idea, for while Hungary, Bohemia, Cracow and much else did in fact belong to the realm, Jerusalem, Toscana and many others in the list certainly did not.

The Viennese population mirrors the fact that Vienna was the centre of a wide region with a great many nationalities. To this day Viennese surnames are a captivating and enlightening mixture of local and immigrant strains. Looking at Viennese shop signs is an ethnological adventure, the Viennese telephone directory ridicules any idea of racial purity, in particular under Po- (Pochvalevsky, Poczymek, Podaril, Podbrany, Podebradsky, Podeschwa, Podgaischek, Podgornik, Podhradsky, Podhrajsek, Pogatschnik etc.), under Vy- (Vybiral, Vybrny, Vycesal, Vychitil, Vycudil, Vymlatyl, Vyoralek, Vyplasil, Vyskocil, Vystrcil etc.) but also under Sm-, Sr-, Chl- and Chm. And something like that was to be annexed to a *"großdeutsches Reich"!*

Vienna was the capital of an entity and of an idea which included Bohemia and Slovakia, Carpato Russia and Hungary, Bukovina and half of Poland, Krain, Croatia, Trieste und Dalmatia, part of Lago Maggiore and much else besides. The pattern of the city of two million inhabitants corresponded to that function. Since November 1918, however, that selfsame Vienna has been the capital of a Republic with a total of about seven million inhabitants, reduced for the first time since time immemorial to the reality of a definitive constitutional area, and not out of its own free will but rather as the victim of a dictated treaty. "L'Autriche, c'est ce qui reste", Georges Clémenceau had said. What remained after Hungary had been separated, after Czechoslovakia had constituted itself, after the South Slavs had united, after Romania and Italy had helped themselves to chunks of territory, that became Austria. The absurd method of that peace solution, the proclamation of a republic without any preparation, the relationship between a giant city and a dwarf state, these were things that could not be mastered within a day. It may even have been a historical and psychological necessity that the precarious reality was doomed to extinction between 1938 and 1945.

Vienna had never been quite real as the capital of the Republic of Austria. And then in the Second Republic it experienced a resurrection as though it had always been there.

That Vienna has become neither too large nor too small for itself and remained identical with itself, true to its past as the Imperial capital and residence but not restorative, that it could fulfil its role as the centre of a federalistically constituted Alpine Republic, in a word that Vienna still is Vienna seems to me a remarkable achievement and would suggest that Austria in its present form is not only the result of the dictate of the victorious powers of 1918 but rather a meaningful entity, that everything else that was larger was merely the shell and that the country between Lake Constance and Lake Neusiedl was always the core. Otherwise Vienna could not have proved itself twice under the most difficult post-war conditions.

Perhaps the rebirth of Vienna in the Second Republic will at one time enter history not only as a "good old time" but rather as a great time. Such thoughts are of course unpopular and very much foreign to the spirit of Vienna. They are, however, suggested by the fact that there was at no time any serious monarchist movement in the Austrian Republic, despite the fact that such ideas would certainly have had a certain allure after centuries as a great power. The Republic could even afford to tolerate the erection of a Franz-Josef-Memorial in the old Emperor's Garden, now the *Burggarten.* It is so deeply anchored in reality and in the consciousness of the people, so obviously above question, that the very term "Republic of Austria" is generally left to stamps, coins and courts of law.

Great as our second post-war period may seem to those who come after us, it will at best be considered the second greatest of the great epochs of Vienna. The greatest was without doubt the epoch from the middle of the 18th century to the Napoleonic wars: during the Baroque period idea and reality merged — wholeness came into the world from Vienna when symphonic music originated here.

Baroque and symphonic music live in close neighbourhood just outside the Ring, in a somewhat larger second arc which is called *Lastenstrasse,* a name for which one will search in vain on street signs. It is also known as the *Zweierlinie* despite the fact the "2" tram has long been discontinued. Close to the Opera there is the *Karlsplatz,* a large area without any real enclosures and with quite a few attractions, for instance the *Jugendstil* stations of the *Stadtbahn* by the great architect Otto Wagner or the Museum of the City of Vienna hiding behind trees. There is much greenery, and the fine arts also have two homes here: the *Künstlerhaus* (artists' house) and the *Secession,* neighbours to music which resides in the *Musikverein,* the *Konzerthaus* and the Academy of Music. And there is St. Charles' itself. Whatever has been done, is being done or might be done to this square: St. Charles' has an indestructably ideal position, like the central object of an exhibition, the whole concept centring round that position as though the meaning of a church lay not so much in being visited as being looked at, as though the service lay in the view itself, as though the essence of the church was fulfilled in its cupola. St. Charles' is after all not much more than a position and a cupola attractively flanked by two Roman Trajan's columns and two little towers.

Close by (these squares can almost be considered communicating vessels) is the *Schwarzenbergplatz* with the only disfigurement of the city of which Vienna is innocent: the Russian monument which obstructs the view of the Schwarzenberg Palace, an artistic failure forced upon Vienna by the State Treaty. From here the land rises to one of those gentle hills which enliven and vary the structure of the city. This hill — we are going approximately due South from the centre — is the most important. On its crest, quite close to the Southern Station, lies the Belvedere Palace in its severe, almost ascetic, garden which descends in terraces. It is a palace with two front façades, two garden fronts of different but equally perfect character, one facing the city and its terraces privileged with a unique view. Still in the middle of the city one yet sees the city below one to the edge of the Vienna Woods, as though the Belvedere had not been placed there because of the view but rather as though the city and its surroundings had been cunningly composed from this vantage point.

St. Charles' — the Belvedere — the National Library in the Hofburg complex with its large ceremonial hall which seems somehow familiar to everyone because it has so often been photographed, drawn, painted and filmed — and *Schönbrunn* Palace — they would suffice to raise the city to the noble rank of beautiful cities.

If we break off again and turn West towards Schönbrunn now, we are justified by the analogy that Schönbrunn, like the Belvedere, has no back, thus degrading its distant cousin Versailles with its not very attractive "town front" to the position of a poor relation. The two façades of Schönbrunn, the town and the garden fronts, are totally different — as are those of the Belvedere — and only matched by their respective opposites. The triumph of perfection goes so far that a complementing structure, the Gloriette, was placed on the hill opposite the garden front, a hill which almost looks as though it had been erected there for that very purpose, without any other function than that of being seen, a resting point for the eye, a view *per se*. And as though the two dual palaces themselves wanted to be complementary, the Belvedere also has a pendant flattering to the eye, in this case not raised but closing off the ascetic garden as a noble smaller replica of the Palace.

We have again come close to the centre, the Ring and the *Zweierlinie,* the core of Vienna, the "city". We are within the inner one-digit districts. Belvedere Palace and Garden lie on the border between the third and fourth districts. The fifth to ninth districts follow in clockwise numerical order, long urbanized and yet retaining many relics of a former village character; some, for instance, still have their own "high street". And thus in a sense the first district of Vienna has in fact remained "the city" of former days, more or less closely interwoven with other communities which yet retain a certain amount of autonomy, small towns or villages or valleys or riparian meadows, e.g. Leopoldstadt (2nd district), Floridsdorf (21st district), Brigittenau (20th district).

The 2nd and 20th districts have a special position, lying on an island between the Danube on the outer and the Danube Canal on the city side. The Danube Canal branches off from the Danube above Vienna and joins it again below the city. What could not have become of that tolerably imposing waterway — it is about as large as the Spree in Berlin — if it had brought an even slightly more attractive name into its marriage with the city of Vienna! Magic, atmosphere, even poetry it doubtless has, and they would have been praised in poetry and song, it would have become popular and legendary — but it has forfeited it all because of its name. Nobody sings the praises of a canal.

The facelessness of the island today is due to the fact that Leopoldstadt and Brigittenau were predominantly Jewish quarters. The Viennesse poet Ilse Aichinger conjured up that world for the last time in her novel *"Die größere Hoffnung"* (The greater hope) and symbolized its end in the destruction of a bridge from the Leopoldstadt into the "city".

The bridges across the Danube Canal have long been restored, but it is still not quite clear just where they do lead from the city. Very gradually a new modern district is a rising here from a virtual vacuum, a centre beside the centre. A significant step in this direction was the new planning concept for the *Praterstern.* This shows the face of modern Vienna in its claim for generous solutions. Here again, however, it is the lay-out of the roads, the landscaping, the pavements and the underpasses which are successful while the design of the streetlamps and houses is questionable. In any case, the houses are not a dominating feature round the *Praterstern.* This is the place of transition from the city to the *Prater* which is part of the city and yet also a distant, secret landscape, beginning at a city square and reaching far beyond the borders of the city.

The *Prater* is no park, no garden, no wood, no riparian landscape, no fun-fair, it is rather a unique synthesis of all these elements, so huge that the *Wurstelprater* with its stalls, its roundabouts, its shooting galleries, its grotto railways, its helter-skelters, the Ferris Wheel and many, many other attractions together with a variety of restaurants, outdoor beer gardens and refreshment kiosks is a world in itself and yet only a small sector of the Prater. Even the two race courses, the large stadium for almost 100,000 spectators and the beautiful outdoor pool, the exhibition grounds round the *"Rotunde"* (which is no longer round) make no real inroads on this gigantic area where meadows, tree-lined avenues, riparian forests, ponds and river arms reach down to the Danube, where a few minutes' drive away from the city one yet feels far away and enchanted.

Here at last the city meets its river, and on leaving the city it blesses it. Mountains and hills are forgotten, here is the great plain into which Vienna reaches and grows, which the river enters after marking the border between the end of the Alpine range and the first foothills of the Carpathians above the city. This is riverside country, riparian landscape, width. It has been said (and is frequently quoted to this day) that the Balkans begin a few steps away from the *Schwarzenbergplatz* in the third district. One might equally say that while Vienna is wholly part of Central Europe, the *Prater* belongs to Eastern Europe.

The transition to the Balkans (the quotation is attributed to State Chancellor Metternich) takes place "on the *Landstrasse*". Needless to say the *Landstrasse* is by no means a country road as the name implies but rather the third district of Vienna which starts with feudal palaces, gardens and metropolitan traffic routes and gradually becomes suburban, even takes on a village character with those typical rows of low houses which make the East of Austria so very Eastern — Balkan in fact.

One realizes how large the city is when one goes from the Ring through that third district and then through the eleventh to the huge Central Cemetary and then out to Vienna's elegant airport. The drive in the opposite direction is less impressive and yet quite representative. The city unfolds in an evolutionary process as it were, almost biogenetically step by step developing from village to suburb, showing its anonymous, densely settled width before it attains its Imperial image just before one reaches the Ring. That also is Vienna: the endless grey faceless reservoir of the suburbs, the city of "rent barracks" spreading on all sides where the hills of the Vienna Woods do not act as a dam.

Yet even here Vienna is not quite conventional, not quite like any other city. In these outer districts we find, first of all, the municipal housing estates, a different kind of Viennese speciality. In the 'twenties the municipality followed a radical housing policy, among other ambitious and important achievements under Social Democratic leadership, above all under the great mayor Karl Seitz and his assistants Breitner, Glöckel and Tandler. A price stop called "rent protection" artificially kept rents down. Since the First World War anyone who could retain an old apartment has paid unrealistically cheap rents. The rents in the municipal flats were also kept at an artifcially low level. In their day the huge housing estates were radical and revolutionary not only from a sociopolitical but also from an architectural point of view. After 1945, however, a slightly modernized version of the rent barracks was also thrown up.

Property has not produced any income in Vienna since 1919, which accounts for the pitiable state of many older apartment houses. This neglect, side by side with costly new private apartment houses, is one aspect of the image of the city.

In the middle of the rows of houses in the large suburban reservoir, however, one keeps finding relics of the old, lively, characteristic and traditional individuality of the district. The city did not — as in America — grow into a vacuum but rather embraced a village, a region, a particular landscape, as e.g. the Lichtental (in the ninth district) where Schubert was born, or the Ulrichsgrund (in the seventh district) round the church where Gluck got married and where Joseph Lanner and Johann Strauss Junior were born.

Apart from their common centre, the Viennese are very much inhabitants of a particular quarter and feel like strangers outside their native village or valley, almost uprooted. We have long given up any systematic presentation of the progression from the second to the ninth district, and it would indeed be most un-Viennese to portray the city in pedantic classification. We just must point out that unity is the result of diversity here, which has also found its way into literature. One might indeed speak of a literary federalism within the city, with the great Viennese Arthur Schnitzler not presenting "Vienna" but rather particular districts (with a preference for his native 18th district), and the great chronicler of more recent Vienna, Heimito von Doderer, lovingly turning his attention at his immediate neighbourhood, the ninth district. In literature, too, the first district forms the common denominator.

Mariahilfer Strasse plays a particular role within the one-digit districts (lying between the sixth and the seventh) as a large shopping street. What seems too expensive "in the city" one might find more cheaply "in Mariahilf"; here too, the kitsch orgies of Christmas lights and decorations reach their climax.

The centrifugal tendency of trade incidentally also reached Vienna some time back, huge shopping centres with parking facilities being built on the outskirts and advertised so intensively and made so attractive that parking will soon become a problem out there as well.

We must not quite ignore the eighth district *(Josefstadt)* because it offers two magnificent halls: the *Jodok-Fink* square in front of the Piarist church and the *Theater in der Josefstadt,* Vienna's most beautiful theatre, for which Beethoven wrote *Die Weihe des Hauses* and which Max Reinhardt adapted — restoring the old style rather than renovating it — and opened in 1924 as his Viennese theatre. At that time it was daring not to be architecturally daring. We owe a timelessly splendid theatre in good old style to that decision.

The ninth district, *Alsergrund,* finishes the inner arc of the districts. Here there is not only the beautiful *Strudlhofstiege* which Doderer immortalized, here we find a particular cosmos within the city, twisting village lanes in Schubert's *Lichtenthal,* metropolitan traffic routes, suburban business and a city within the city: university institutes, clinics, hospitals — an "academic quarter".

We have now come back to the Danube Canal from which we started and we recognize that the topography is by no means accidental but rather systematic: round the core of the inner city the districts two to nine form a clockwise arc.

These districts are bordered by an outer "ring", the Gürtel (belt), a very wide, generous "outer boulevard", which needless to say is no proper belt since it is not closed upon itself. Outside the *Gürtel* the districts ten and above again form an arc. For a long time there was a total of twenty-one, the 22nd and a 23rd districts being added rather late.

Only two, the 21st and 22nd districts, lie on the other side of the Danube, which does not really belong to the city at all and is further isolated by a broad strip of unbuilt land, the inundation area. For all those who do not actually live beside it, the Danube is far outside, not part of the city but rather a far-off destination. For the time being this is only theoretically and officially Vienna, a truly organic part of the city is only gradually coming into being. As yet there are a few scattered islands of future urbanity, industrial and housing estates within a sea of open country, suburb, village and the paradise of riparian landscape and Danube arms, including the city's super-beach *Gänsehäufel* (goose mound).

This jump across the Danube has taken us far beyond our immediate destination on our progress through Vienna. We had just reached the *Gürtel,* which ought to enclose the inner, one-digit districts but only separates them from the two-digit districts in a large unfinished arc.

Beyond the *Gürtel* the progressive topographical clockwise "chronology" is still retained, but whatever problematic unity and uniformity one has been able to trace so far now gives way to an orgy of diversity. This is due to the fact that the city of Vienna lies on an edge, that after *Ring* and *Gürtel* a farthest arc surrounds the city, the range of hills which reaches from the vineyards of *Nußdorf* in the North-West to those of *Perchtoldsdorf* in the South and opens towards the great plains in the North, East and South.

The Alps reach from the French Mediterranean coast to *Heiligenstadt, Nußdorf, Grinzing, Sievering, Salmannsdorf, Neuwaldegg, Hütteldorf, Lainz, Mauer, Perchtoldsdorf.* The Eastern European plain reaches from the Urals to the *Prater,* to *Schwechat, Kaisermühlen, Floridsdorf, Stadlau.* With the "nose" of the *Leopoldsberg* the Alps drop steeply to the Danube. The Carpathians only send their furthest delegate to the left bank of the Danube: the *Bisamberg,* which, however, only gives character to the plain without really interrupting it.

The miniature mountains of the Vienna Woods descend towards the city, they structure its furthest outposts into valleys with village streets between vineyards which have retained much of their character and homeliness — even if somewhat self-consciously for the purpose of attractiveness. For here in the suburbs facing "Franz-Josef", West and South, is the home of the *Heuriger,* meaning both the new wine and the places where that new wine is drunk. In principle at least this wine is sold by the vintners themselves, and where the *Heuriger* is genuine it has to be primitive, almost archaic, with wooden tables and benches in a sloping garden and an unornamented primitive room, not a restaurant like any other, and definitely without noisy music. But for the sake of attractiveness the *"Nobelheurige"* are appointed the way the uninitiated would like to find them, with artificial "atmosphere" and overintensive music.

The houses, however, their courtyards, the narrow lanes out there are genuine, very much part of the landscape, which is gentle and friendly. Beethoven's *Pastorale* seems to have composed them and is probably partly to be blamed for the legend of Viennese gentleness and graciousness. It is waiting just beyond the importuning musical background, one only has to climb or drive a bit higher, to the *Kobenzl, Kahlenberg, Leopoldsberg,* to the *Her-*

mannskogel or to the *Häuserl am Roa* and to look down on the spread of the city. This is how the liberating army saw the city in 1683 before it descended for the decisive battle when Vienna, besieged by the Turks, saved the Occident, not for the first and not for the last time.

Time and again geography has made history in and around Vienna. This was always an outpost, a centre at the very edge, even at the time of the Romans civilized Europe only just reached past Vienna. The place was called Vindobona then. The name is said to go back to the tribe of the Wendes, but it is much more likely to have something to do with the traditional strong Viennese wind, another doubtful blessing of the city's geographic position.

No, the districts beyond the *Gürtel* cannot be coerced or forced into any kind of meaningful uniformity. Vienna is no city, but rather a sort of "federated villages". Thus for instance there are two rival, thoroughly autonomous and different centres of solid upper middle-class residential areas with old-style villas: *Döbling* and *Währing* (Schnitzler country) on the one hand and on the other *Hietzing* and *Lainz* adjoining the park of *Schönbrunn*. In some quiet oases out there one might think that the late Imperial days were still alive and that they were good days.

Beyond the *Gürtel,* close to the Western Station, also lies the huge Vienna City Hall, surprisingly successful as a work of architecture, a large complex with halls of all kinds for events ranging from bicycle races via Peter Alexander to Mahler symphonies.

It is quite right and just that the Vienna City Hall is primarily devoted to artistic and sporting events and that the municipality, in its efforts to establish its hold on the city, devotes much attention to these events in a hall that is representative for the city. "Circuses" are indeed daily bread in Vienna. Reality has always been overcome and negated here in games and in pomp and circumstance, whether in the theatre, in music, in ball games or formal balls, or processions for Corpus Christi, the First of May — not to forget playing with words and ideas.

Pomp and play and sport and everything sublimely purposeless were and are more highly esteemed and more central here than elsewhere. When one of the leading *Burgtheater* actors dies, his coffin is carried round the theatre in solemn procession — traffic is diverted from the Ringstrasse out of consideration for this ceremony — and nobody in Vienna is surprised or finds this excessive. Artistic and sporting events and affairs frequently make the headlines of the daily papers, they are more passionately discussed than elsewhere. The population of Vienna consists of an audience of almost two million.

The destruction of the State Opera by bombs and of the *Burgtheater* by bivouacking Red Army soldiers were an occasion of sorrow for the whole city, the festive re-opening became a folk festival, and those who had never been inside either house joined in both the sorrow and the festivities.

If at times interest in internal politics rises surprisingly and for brief periods overshadows everything else, then it is in the face of elections which are followed passionately on the radio, on television and in public squares because they, too, are competitive games with uncertain results. Most obligingly, the two large parties, the Reds and the Blacks (Socialists and Christian Democrats) have made sure in the decades of the Second Republic that the election-circuses remained exciting and the result uncertain, indeed there have been two winners and two losers twice, with one party (the Reds) winning more votes and the other (the Blacks) more mandates.

Recently a new kind of game has joined Vienna's traditional preoccupations: television plays, which may actually be a discussion, documentation, information, report or television play in the narrower sense.

However, the relationship between Vienna and that which stirs Vienna is by no means direct and straightforward and one way. We need only think of the River Wien which seems so harmless and can become so dangerous; or of those Viennese who in 1927 set fire to the Palace of Justice and hindered the fire brigade from quenching the fire. Or think of the fact that the sale of bottled drinks is prohibited at football matches because the spectators had a habit of throwing the bottles onto the field in their wrath.

Vienna is great in protest, in negation, in opposition. Relationships with the arts and with sports and politics also frequently go via negation. Even Vienna's identity with itself often takes the form of Vienna questioning itself. (After Franz Grillparzer's funeral Ferdinand Kürnberger wrote: " 'Such things can only be possible in Vienna' is the sterotype reaction when Senatus Populusque Vindobonensis has presented a surprised world with some outrageous villainy, stupidity or tactlessness. But those who say that are again — Vienna.") The allegedly merry, blissful, vivacious, carefree city is the capital of negation, a capital with surprisingly little self-confidence (on the positive side: surprisingly much self-criticism). "Typically Viennese" or "just like Vienna", which would elsewhere certainly be positive epithets, always imply criticism of Vienna without further qualification.

Shatteringly large numbers of great Viennese minds have been negative, destructive and denigratory, and constructive only by detours. Johann Nestroy, Karl Kraus and Ödön von Horváth destroyed their surroundings through presenting them with a satirical mirror-image and thus made them immortal. Arnold Schönberg and Sigmund Freud liquidated the music and the psychology of the 19th century in Vienna. They and others — one might say all truly great creative Viennese — have in turn been denied recognition, been persecuted, negated and ignored by Vienna.

Since the time the Baroque buildings and the great symphonies were finished the greatness of Vienna must be sought in the unfinished, in the disturbed relationship between potential and realization, in denied fulfilment, in the trend towards the fragmentary. Vienna's creative greatness is fulfilled — if at all — against Vienna or outside Vienna. The city of twelve-tone music and psychoanalysis has relatively fewer twelve-tone composers and psychoanalists than other capitals of music and depth psychology.

On the other hand, the number of coffee-houses is still remarkable. Anyone who is inclined to believe the Viennese lament about the dying coffee-house should consult the Viennese telephone directory, which is most elucidating in this context, too. The well-known Viennese carelessness and disorganisation are also still at home in Vienna.

There is a connection between these two statements, and one has to learn to understand Vienna in this context.

The particular Vindobonensian carelessness and disorganization are not, like their counterparts in other regions, an expression of an inability to create order and to realize precision but rather the result of an unwillingness to make use of the requisite faculties. Vienna has frequently shown that it can be efficient and hard-working (most recently in the ordeals after the Second World War under the energetic leadership of Theodor Körner, the mayor during the period of deprivation, and in the reconstruction of the city under severe outer and inner difficulties). Vienna can be if it wants to, or rather: Vienna could be if it wanted to. But Vienna does not always wish to want to. Vienna is quite well satisfied in the knowledge that it could be. The possibility attains an absolute quality and substitutes for the realization. The idea stands for the result. It works this way, too. And the simple fact that Vienna exists while these lines are written and read, as a comparatively prospering capital of an exceedingly stable republic, with a comparatively high standard of social justice and a minimum of inner and social unrest, this very fact triumphantly confirms this Viennese creed: It works this way, too.

Elsewhere leisure is a welcome break from work. In Vienna work is an unwelcome break from leisure. Most important is play, the play of thoughts augmented by wine at the *Heuriger,* by coffee in the coffee-house. In the coffee-house thoughts are alive and meet in a game with reality. Sometimes a Viennese is taken from the coffee-house and becomes a great man. Usually, however, he is satisfied with a conjunctivistic attitude to life: one should, one ought to, one could. Usually he says no to his environment, to Vienna, to himself. If he writes his No down, if he composes or paints it or organizes it into a meaningful system, the world is lucky. More frequently, however, he finds fulfilment in a game of ideas, at best in a joke.

That is why the Viennese do not really like going away from Vienna. They want to negate Vienna. And when abroad they find themselves longing for Vienna and having to say yes to Vienna. All those who are far from Vienna think of their city with a special kind of homesickness. They want to be back where, while they cannot be happy, they can be rather more pleasantly, more lustily unhappy — and in the very best company.

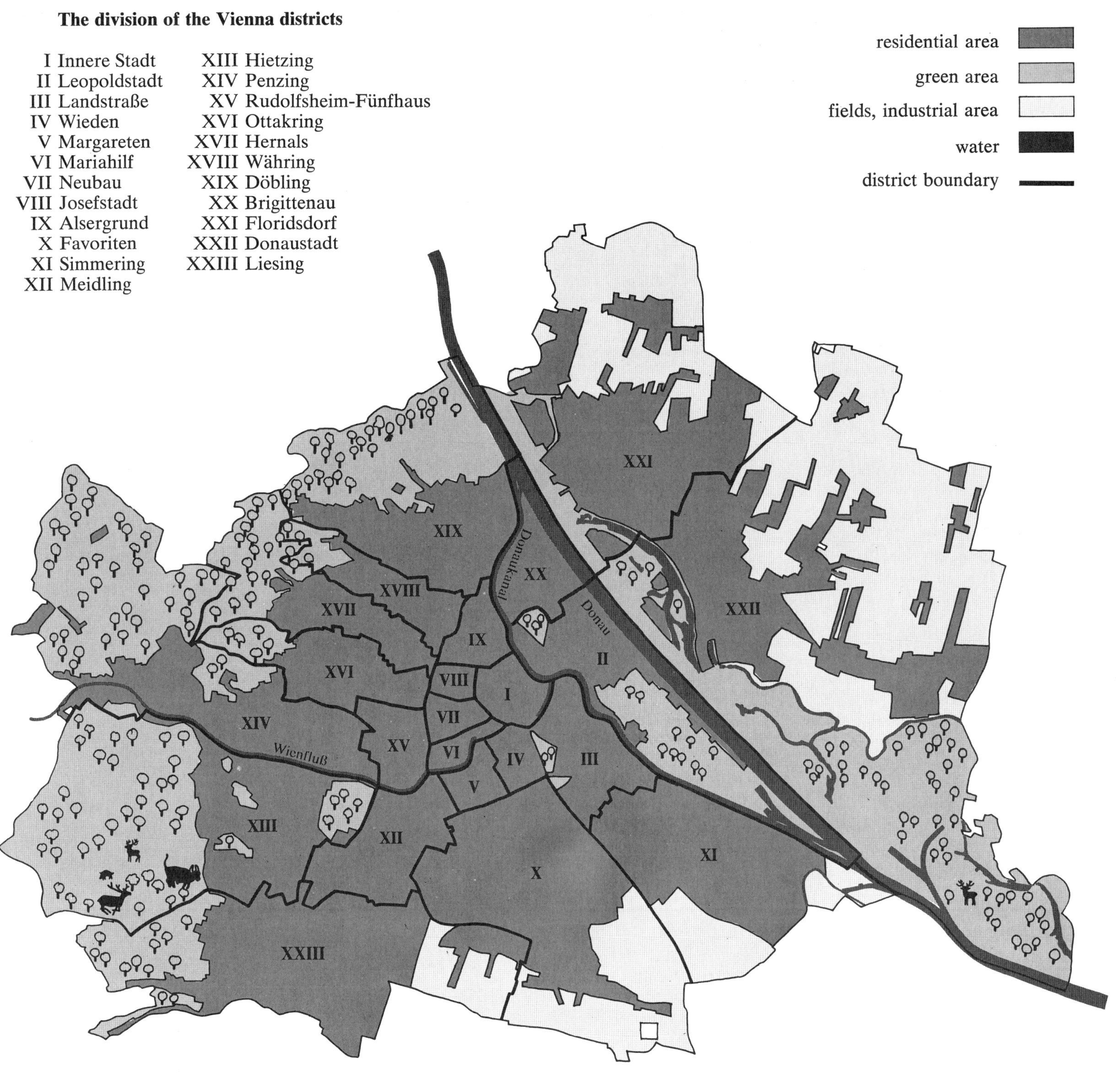
The division of the Vienna districts
I Innere Stadt
II Leopoldstadt
III Landstraße
IV Wieden
V Margareten
VI Mariahilf
VII Neubau
VIII Josefstadt
IX Alsergrund
X Favoriten
XI Simmering
XII Meidling
XIII Hietzing
XIV Penzing
XV Rudolfsheim-Fünfhaus
XVI Ottakring
XVII Hernals
XVIII Währing
XIX Döbling
XX Brigittenau
XXI Floridsdorf
XXII Donaustadt
XXIII Liesing
residential area
green area
fields, industrial area
water
district boundary
Donaukanal
Donau
Wienfluß

A few facts about Vienna

The federal capital Vienna is both a province and a municipality. Thus the mayor is also the provincial governor, the city senate the provincial government and the city council the provincial diet. The city council has 100 members, who are elected every five years.
The city covers an area of 414 sq. km and has a perimeter of 133 km.
St. Stephen's Square: 48° 14' 54" Northern latitude, 16° 21' 42" Eastern longitude, 171 m above the Adriatic.
Lowest point: the Lobau, 151 m; highest point: Hermannskogel, 542 m.
1,614,841 inhabitants (1971 census); 902,473 female, 712,368 male.
A total of 804,283 apartments, 200,140 of which are administered by the municipality.

Culture:
14 theatres, 7 concert halls, 13 small stages, 93 cinemas, 17 state museums, 14 municipal museums, 26 other museums, 8 collections of the National Library, 21 exhibition rooms.
Libraries:
National Library with 2.18 million volumes, University Library with 1.81 million volumes, Library of the Technical University with 367,000 volumes, Vienna City and Provincial Libarary with 289,000 volumes, Municipal Libraries with 654,000 volumes.
In the school year 1975/76:
241 primary schools, 136 secondary schools (including polytechnical courses), 44 special schools, 35 vocational secondary schools, 78 intermediate vocational schools, 26 training colleges (including pedagogical academies), 79 general high schools, University, Technical University, University of Economics, Agricultural University, Veterinary University, colleges of art, Vienna City Conservatory, 14 adult education centres.

Recreation:
109 sports grounds, covering 4.33 million sq. m, 662 games and tennis grounds covering 1.24 million sq. m. 6 municipal swimming halls, 25 municipal baths, 15 municipal open-air swimming pools, 32 open-air children's pools. Lainz Deer Park with 25 sq. km; 17.4 sq. km of public gardens.
Tourism:
275 hotels and pensions, 3.6 million nights booked, 3.1 million by foreigners.
Traffic:
485,000 registered vehicles, 404,000 of which are private cars.
Vienna-Schwechat Airport: 43,000 arrivals and departures, 2.2 million passengers.
Danube shipping: 148,000 passengers.
Economy:
Gross product for Viennese industry in 1975 was 59.4 milliard schillings; 784,000 employees (at the end of 1975).

Figures from the Statistical Office of the City of Vienna, as of 1975.

Cover picture
View from the square Am Hof towards St. Stephen's

Main title, page 3
Wrought iron gate at the Upper Belvedere

Section title, page 5
Coat of arms on the façade of the Old Town Hall in Wipplingerstrasse

Section title, page 17
Cupola of the Michaeler Wing of the New Hofburg

Index of sources of pictures

Picture archives of the Austrian National Library
Plate 4

Vienna Tourist Association, archives
Plates 3, 23, 87

Peter Hassmann
Cover, section title, page 17,
plates 5, 6, 7, 8, 9, 10, 15, 17, 18, 19, 20, 21, 22, 24, 25, 26, 27, 28, 29, 30, 31 32, 35, 36, 37, 38, 39, 40, 42, 43, 44, 55, 57, 58, 62, 63, 64, 65, 68, 71, 73, 74, 75, 76, 77, 78, 79, 81, 82, 83, 84, 85, 89, 93, 95, 96, 98, 102, 103, 106, 108, 111, 112, 113, 114, 115, 118, 119, 120, 121, 123, 125, 126, 127, 128, 129, 130, 131, 132, 133, 134, 136, 137, 139, 140, 141, 142, 143, 144, 147, 148, 149

Ernst Hausner
Main title, section title, page 5,
plates 1, 2, 11, 12, 13, 14, 34, 41, 46, 47, 48, 49, 50, 51, 53, 54, 56, 59, 60, 61, 80, 88, 91, 94, 97, 99, 100, 101, 104, 105, 107, 109, 110, 122, 135, 145, 146, 150

Vienna Provincial Picture Department
Plate 90

Gerhard Markowitsch
Plates 16, 67, 69, 70, 92, 117

Helmut Partaj
Plates 72, 86, 138

Barbara Pflaum
Plates 45, 66, 116, 124

Josefstadt Theatre, archives
Plate 33

Franz Vogler
Plate 52

1 Barocke Bauten in der Wiener Innenstadt: Kurrentgasse.
2 Altbauensemble mit Teilen aus der Gotik: Griechengasse.
3 Einer der ältesten Stadtteile Wiens: Blutgasse.
4 Vogelschauplan der Stadt Wien von Joseph Daniel Huber, 1769.
5 und 6 Stephansdom, Mittelschiff.

Die Stephanskirche stammt in ihren Anfängen aus der ersten Hälfte des 12. Jahrhunderts. Der gotische Bau entstand im wesentlichen im 14. und im 15. Jahrhundert, der 136,7 m hohe Südturm wurde 1433 vollendet.

1 Baroque buildings in the centre of Vienna: Kurrentgasse.
2 Old buildings, partly Gothic: Griechengasse.
3 One of the oldest quarters of Vienna: Blutgasse.
4 Bird's eye view of the city of Vienna by Joseph Daniel Huber, 1769.
5 and 6 St. Stephen's Cathedral, nave.

St. Stephen's goes back to the first half of the 12th century. The Gothic structure was built mainly in the 14th and 15th centuries, the 136.7 metre South tower was completed in 1433.

1 Bâtiments baroques dans le centre de la ville de Vienne: Kurrentgasse.
2 Ensemble de bâtiments anciens de style gothique: Griechengasse.
3 Un des quartiers les plus anciens de Vienne: Blutgasse.
4 Vue à vol d'oiseau de la ville de Vienne de Joseph Daniel Huber, 1769.
5 et 6 Cathédrale Saint-Etienne, nef centrale.

Les débuts de la construction de l'église Saint-Etienne datent de la première moitié du 12ème siècle. L'église obtint surtout son caractère gothique durant les 14ème et 15ème siècles; la tour Sud haute de 136,7 mètres fut terminée en 1433.

1 Costruzioni barocche nel centro storico di Vienna: Kurrentgasse.
2 Gruppo di antichi edifici con elementi gotici: Griechengasse.
3 Uno dei più antichi quartieri di Vienna: Blutgasse.
4 Piano a volo d'uccello della città di Vienna di J. D. Huber, 1769.
5 e 6 Duomo di Santo Stefano, navata centrale. L'inizio della chiesa di

Santo Stefano risale alla prima metà del secolo XII. La parte gotica fu costruita principalmente nei secoli XIV e XV, la torre sud, alta 136,7 metri fu completata nel 1433.

1

2

3

Q
P

7 Bürgerhaus „Zum blauen Karpfen“ (Annagasse 14), Bauwerk des 17. Jahrhunderts mit klassizistischer Fassade (1814).
8 Im barocken Bürgerhaus Bäckerstraße 16 befand sich im vorigen Jahrhundert ein Gasthaus mit dem Namen „Schmauswaberl“.
9 Portal der „Böhmischen Hofkanzlei“, Wipplingerstraße 7, erbaut 1708—1714 nach Plänen von Johann Bernhard Fischer von Erlach.
10 Portal des Palais Erdödy-Fürstenberg, Himmelpfortgasse 13, erbaut um 1724, Architekt unbekannt.
11—14 Barocker Fassadenschmuck an Wiener Bürgerhäusern.
15 Renaissance-Portal der Salvatorkirche, Salvatorgasse 5.
16 Das Palais Obizzi am Schulhof, Ende des 17. Jahrhunderts im barocken Stil errichtet, beherbergt das Uhrenmuseum der Stadt Wien.
17 Treppenhaus des Palais Kinsky, Freyung 4, 1713—1716 von Johann Lukas von Hildebrandt für Generalfeldzeugmeister Graf Daun erbaut.

7 Burgher's house “Zum blauen Karpfen” (At the sign of the Blue Carp —Annagasse 14), 17th century building with Classicist façade (1814).
8 During the last century the Baroque burgher's house Bäckerstraße 16 housed an inn by the name of “Schmauswaberl” (Feast-wench).
9 Portal of the “Bohemian Court Chancellery”, Wipplingerstraße 7, built 1708—1714 to plans by Johann Bernhard Fischer von Erlach.
10 Portal of Palais Erdödy-Fürstenberg, Himmelpfortgasse 13, built ca. 1724 by an unknown architect.
11—14 Baroque decorations on Viennese burghers' houses.
15 Renaissance portal of the Salvator Church, Salvatorgasse 5.
16 Palais Obizzi on Schulhof, built towards the end of the 17th century in Baroque style, houses the Clock Museum of the City of Vienna.
17 Entrance hall of Palais Kinsky, Freyung 4, built 1713—1716 by Johann Lukas von Hildebrandt for commander-in-chief Graf Daun.

7 Maison bourgeoise baroque «A la carpe bleue», Annagasse No 14, bâtiment du 17ème siècle à façade classique (1814).
8 Dans la maison baroque au No 16 de la Bäckerstraße se trouvait au siècle dernier une auberge du nom de «Schmauswaberl» (bonne femme gourmande).
9 Portail de la Chancellerie de Bohème, Wipplingerstraße No 7, construite de 1708 à 1714 d'après les plans de Johann Bernhard Fischer von Erlach.
10 Portail du palais Erdödy-Fürstenberg, Himmelpfortgasse No 13, construit en 1724, architecte inconnu.
11—14 Décorations baroques des façades de maisons bourgeoises de Vienne.
15 Portail de style Renaissance de l'église du Saint-Sauveur, Salvatorgasse No 5.
16 Le palais Obizzi sur le Schulhof, construit dans le style baroque à la fin du 17ème siècle, renferme le Musée des Horloges de la Ville de Vienne.
17 Escalier du palais Kinsky, Freyung No 4, construit de 1713 à 1716 par Johann Lukas von Hildebrandt pour le comte Daun, général en chef des armées.

7 Casa «Zum blauen Karpfen» (alla carpa blu), Annagasse 14, costruzione del secolo XVII con facciata classicista (1814).
8 Nel secolo scorso in questa casa borghese barocca nella Bäckerstraße 16 c'era un'albergo che portava il nome «Schmauswaberl».
9 Portale della «Böhmische Hofkanzlei» (Cancelleria di Corte Boema) nella Wipplingerstraße 7 costruito nel 1708—1714 su progetto di Johann Bernhard Fischer von Erlach.
10 Portale del Palazzo Erdödy-Fürstenberg nella Himmelpfortgasse 13 costruito intorno al 1724 da un architetto sconosciuto.
11—14 Ornamento barocco di facciata delle case borghesi viennesi.
15 Portale rinascimentale della Salvatorkirche nella Salvatorgasse 5.
16 Il Palazzo Obizzi nello Schulhof, costruito alla fine del secolo XVII in stile barocco, ospita il museo degli orologi della città di Vienna.
17 Vano delle scale del Palazzo Kinsky nella Freyung 4 costruito nel 1713—1716 da Johann Lukas von Hildebrandt per il generale d'armata conte Daun.

7

8

9

10

1

12

3

14

15

UHRENMUSEUM

7

Wichtige und bedeutende Bauwerke und Institutionen befinden sich im Bereich der Gesamtanlage der Wiener Hofburg: der Leopoldinische Trakt, der Schweizerhof mit dem Renaissanceportal, die spätgotische Burgkapelle, die Weltliche und die Geistliche Schatzkammer, die Stallburg, die Österreichische Nationalbibliothek, die Winterreitschule, der Michaelertrakt, die Redoutensäle.

18 Krone des Heiligen Römischen Reiches, aus der zweiten Hälfte des 10. Jahrhunderts. Sie befindet sich in der Weltlichen Schatzkammer.
19 Schauräume im Burgtrakt der „Reichskanzlei".
20 Blick vom Turm des Rathauses zur Neuen Burg.
21 Der Platz „In der Burg" mit dem Denkmal des österreichischen Kaisers Franz I. (als römisch-deutscher Kaiser bis 1806 Franz II.).
22 Österreichische Nationalbibliothek, vormals Hofbibliothek, erbaut 1723—1726 von Vater und Sohn Fischer von Erlach. Prunksaal, mit Deckenfresken von Daniel Gran.
23 Vorführung der Spanischen Reitschule in der von Joseph Emanuel Fischer von Erlach erbauten Winterreitschule in der Burg.

The Wiener Hofburg encompasses many important buildings and institutions: the Leopold Wing, the Swiss courtyard with the Renaissance portal, the late Gothic court chapel, the Temporal and Spiritual Treasury, the Stallburg, the Austrian National Library, the Winter Riding School, the Michaeler Wing, the Redoutensäle.

18 Crown of the Holy Roman Empire, second half of the 10th century. It is kept in the Temporal Treasury.
19 Ceremonial rooms in the "Imperial Chancellery" Wing.
20 View from the Town Hall tower towards the Neue Burg.
21 Square "In der Burg" with the memorial of Austrian Emperor Franz I (until 1806 Franz II as Holy Roman Emperor).
22 Austrian National Library, former court library, built 1723—1726 by Fischer von Erlach father and son. Ceremonial hall, with ceiling frescoes by Daniel Gran.
23 Performance of the Spanish Riding School in the Winter Riding School in the Burg built by Joseph Emanuel Fischer von Erlach.

Des bâtiments et des institutions notables et importants se trouvent dans le complexe de la Hofburg: l'aile Léopold, la Cour des Suisses, la chapelle du château, le Trésor profane et religieux, la Stallburg, la Bibliothèque Nationale Autrichienne, le manège d'hiver, l'aile de Michael, la salle des Redoutes.

18 Couronne du Saint Empire Romain de la 2ème moitié du 10ème siècle. Elle se trouve dans le Trésor de la Couronne.
19 Les appartements dans l'aile de la «Chancellerie d'Empire».
20 Vue de la tour de l'Hôtel de Ville vers le Nouveau Burg.
21 Place «In der Burg» avec le monument de l'empereur d'Autriche François I (empereur romain-germanique jusqu'en 1806 sous le nom de François II).
22 Bibliothèque Nationale Autrichienne, autrefois Bibliothèque de la Cour, construite de 1723 à 1726 par les Fischer von Erlach, père et fils. Grande salle avec fresques de plafond de Daniel Gran.
23 Représentation de l'Ecole d'Equitation Espagnole dans le manège d'hiver construit dans le Burg par Joseph Emanuel von Erlach.

Importanti e significativi edifici ed istituzioni sorgono nell'ambito della Wiener Hofburg (residenza imperiale): l'ala leopoldina; lo Schweizerhof con il portale rinascimentale; la cappella di corte che risale alla tarda epoca gotica; il Tesoro Profano e Sacro; la Stallburg la Biblioteca Nacionale Austriaca; la Scuola d'Equitazione d'Inverno; la Michaelertrakt (l'ala verso la Michaelerplatz); le Redoutensäle.

18 Corona del Sacro Romano Impero della seconda metà del secolo X. Si trova nel Tesoro di Corte profano.
19 Sale nell'ala della Burg che ospitava la cancelleria imperiale.
20 Vista panoramica dalla torre del Municipio verso la Neue Burg.
21 La piazza «In der Burg» col monumento all'Imperatore Austriaco Francesco I (fino al 1806, come Imperatore Romano — Germanico, Francesco II).
22 Biblioteca Nazionale Austriaca, una volta sede della Biblioteca di Corte, costruita nel 1723—1726 dagli architetti Fischer von Erlach padre e figlio. Sala di rappresentanza con affreschi sulla volta di Daniel Gran.
23 Rappresentazione della Scuola Spagnola d'Equitazione nella sede della Scuola d'Equitazione d'Inverno costruita da Joseph Emanuel Fischer von Erlach all'interno della Burg.

18

19

0

1

Zu den Bauwerken, die Wiens Stadtbild mitprägen, gehören viele Kirchen, vor allem aus der Zeit der Gotik — außer der Stephanskirche z. B. Maria am Gestade, Michaelerkirche, Minoritenkirche — und der Barockzeit. Das Stadtbild bestimmen auch die beiden 1872—1881 erbauten großen Museen am Ring mit ihren markanten Kuppeln.

24 Kunsthistorisches Museum, Gemäldegalerie.
25 Naturhistorisches Museum.
26 Kunsthistorisches Museum, Stiegenhaus mit Decken- und Wandgemälden von Michael Munkáczy, Hans Makart, Franz Matsch, Gustav und Ernst Klimt und Antonio Canova.
27 und 28 Peterskirche, erbaut 1703—1708 nach Plänen von Gabriele Montani; Kuppel und Innenraum.
29 und 30 Karlskirche, erbaut 1716—1739 von Vater und Sohn Fischer von Erlach; Kuppel und Innenraum.
31 Piaristenkirche, erbaut zwischen 1716 und 1753 nach Plänen von Johann Lukas von Hildebrandt; Innenraum mit Deckengemälde von Franz Anton Maulbertsch.

Among the buildings which determine the face of the city there are many churches, mainly from the Gothic period—beside St. Stephen's, e.g. Maria am Gestade, St. Michael's, Minoritenkirche—and from the Baroque. The skyline is also dominated by the two large museums on the Ring with their characteristic cupolas, built 1872—1881.

24 Museum of Art History, picture gallery.
25 Museum of Natural History.
26 Museum of Art History, entrance hall with ceiling and wall painting by Michael Munkáczy, Hans Makart, Franz Matsch, Gustav and Ernst Klimt, and Antonio Canova.
27 and 28 St. Peter's, built 1703—1708 to plans by Gabriele Montani; cupola and interior.
29 and 30 St. Charles', built 1716—1739 by Fischer von Erlach father and son; cupola and interior.
31 Piarist Church, built between 1716 and 1753 to plans by Johann Lukas von Hildebrandt; interior with ceiling painting by Franz Anton Maulbertsch.

Aux bâtiments qui donnent à Vienne son caractère, il faut ajouter les nombreuses églises avant tout de style gothique — excepté l'église Saint-Etienne, par ex. Maria am Gestade, l'église Saint-Michel, l'église des Frères Mineurs — et de l'époque baroque. Les deux grands musées construits sur l'avenue du Ring marquent également le caractère de la ville par leurs remarquables coupoles (de 1872 à 1881).

24 Musée d'Histoire de l'Art, galerie de peintures.
25 Musée d'Histoire Naturelle.
26 Musée d'Histoire de l'Art, escalier avec peintures de plafond et murales de Michael Munkáczy, Hans Makart, Franz Matsch, Gustav et Ernst Klimt et Antonio Canova.
27 et 28 Eglise Saint-Pierre, construite de 1703 à 1708 d'après les plans de Gabriele Montani; coupole et intérieur.
29 et 30 Eglise Saint-Charles, construite de 1716 à 1739 par les Fischer von Erlach père et fils; coupole et intérieur.
31 Eglise des Piaristes, construite entre 1716 et 1753 d'après les plans de Johann Lukas von Hildebrandt; intérieur avec peintures de plafond de Franz Maulbertsch.

Tra gli edifici che danno un'impronta alla città si possono annoverare le molte chiese, specialmente quelle risalenti ad epoca gotica — oltre alla chiesa di Santo Stefano, anche la chiesa Maria am Gestade, la Michaelerkirche, la Minoritenkirche — e al periodo barocco. La città è caratterizzata anche dai due grandi musei con le loro spiccate cupole che sorgono sul Ring e che furono costruiti nel 1872—1881.

24 Museo di Storia dell'Arte, Pinacoteca.
25 Museo di Storia Naturale.
26 Museo di Storia dell'Arte, vano delle scale con dipinti sulle pareti e sulla volta di Michael Munkáczy, Hans Makart, Franz Matsch, Gustav e Ernst Klimt e Antonio Canova.
27 e 28 Peterskirche (chiesa di San Pietro), costruita nel 1703—1708 su progetto di Gabriele Montani; cupola e interno.
29 e 30 Karlskirche (chiesa di San Carlo), costruita nel 1716—1739 dagli architetti Fischer von Erlach padre e figlio; cupola e interno.
31 Piaristenkirche (chiesa dei Piaristi), costruita tra il 1716 e il 1753 su progetto di Johann Lukas von Hildebrandt; interno con dipinti sulla volta di Franz Anton Maulbertsch.

24

25

27

29

28

30

32 Burgtheater, am Ring, erbaut 1874—1888 nach Plänen von Carl von Hasenauer und Gottfried Semper.
33 Theater in der Josefstadt, eine Wiener Institution, die sich bis zu Vorläufern ins 18. Jahrhundert zurückverfolgen läßt. 1923 übernahm Max Reinhardt die Leitung der Bühne. Er führte das einstige Vorstadttheater zur Weltgeltung.
34 Theater an der Wien, geht auf eine Gründung im Jahr 1786 zurück und wurde durch Emanuel Schikaneder zu einer der wichtigsten Wiener Vorstadtbühnen. Heute ist das Theater Heimstätte des Musicals und dient auch den Wiener Festwochen und dem Theater der Jugend.
35 und 36 Staatsoper, am Ring, 1861—1869 von August Sicard von Sicardsburg und Eduard van der Nüll erbaut. Das Orchester der Staatsoper sind die Wiener Philharmoniker (36: Opernball).
37 Musikvereinssaal, 1870 von Theophil Hansen erbaut.
38 Der Philharmonikerball im Musikvereinssaal.
39 Der große Konzerthaussaal.
40 Palaiskonzert im Palais Schwarzenberg.

32 Burgtheater, on the Ring, built 1874—1888 to plans by Carl von Hasenauer and Gottfried Semper.
33 Theater in der Josefstadt, a Viennese institution whose roots can be traced back to the 18th century. In 1923 Max Reinhardt took over the direction of the theatre and raised the former suburban stage to world importance.
34 Theater an der Wien, goes back to a foundation of 1787 and became one of the most important Viennese stages outside the centre under Emanuel Schikaneder. Today the theatre is the Viennese home of musicals, and it also serves for the Festival of Vienna and for the Young Peoples' Theatre.
35 and 36 State Opera, on the Ring, built 1861—1869 by August Sicard von Sicardsburg and Eduard van der Nüll. The Vienna Philharmonic Orchestra serves as the State Opera Orchestra (36: Opera Ball).
37 Musikvereinssaal, built 1870 by Theophil Hansen.
38 Ball of the Vienna Philharmonic Orchestra in the Musikvereinssaal.
39 The large hall of the Konzerthaus.
40 Palais concert in the Schwarzenberg Palais.

32 Burgtheater, sur le Ring, construit de 1874 à 1888 d'après les plans de Hasenauer et Gottfried Semper.
33 Théâtre de la Josefstadt, institution viennoise dont on peut suivre les antécédents jusqu'au 18ème siècle. En 1923, Max Reinhardt reprit la direction du théâtre. Il fit de l'ancien théâtre de faubourg une scène de rang mondial.
34 Théâtre an der Wien, date d'une fondation de l'an 1768 et devint grâce à Emanuel Schikaneder une des scènes les plus importantes des faubourgs de Vienne.
35 et 36 L'Opéra National, sur le Ring, construit de 1861 à 1869 par August Sicard von Sicardsburg et Eduard van der Nüll. L'Orchestre Philharmonique de Vienne est l'orchestre attitré de l'Opéra National (36: Bal de l'Opéra).
37 Salle du Musikverein, construite en 1870 par Theophil Hansen.
38 Bal de l'Orchestre Philharmonique dans la salle du Musikverein.
39 La grande salle de la Konzerthaus.
40 Concert au palais Schwarzenberg.

32 Burgtheater, sul Ring; costruito nel 1874—1888 su progetto di Carl von Hasenauer e Gottfried Semper.
33 Teatro nella Josefstadt, un'istituzione viennese i cui precedenti si rintracciano già nel secolo XVIII. Nel 1923 Max Reinhardt assunse la direzione del teatro. Quello che era un teatro di periferia acquistò con lui un importaza mondiale.
34 Teatro an der Wien, la sua costruzione risala all'anno 1786; sotto la direzione di Emanuel Schikaneder divenne uno dei più importanti teatri della periferia. Oggi questo teatro serve per la rappresentazione di commedie musicali e per gli spettacoli del Festival di Vienna e del Theater der Jugend (teatro della gioventù).
35 e 36 Staatsoper, sul Ring, costruita nel 1861—1869 da August Sicard von Sicardsburg e da Eduard van der Nüll. I filarmonici di Vienna compongono l'orchestra della Staatsoper (36: Ballo dell'Opera).
37 Musikvereinssaal (sala da concerti del Musikverein), costruita nel 1870 da Theophil Hansen.
38 Il ballo dei filarmonici nella Musikvereinssaal.
39 Grande sala da concerti della Konzerthaus.
40 Concerto nel Palazzo Schwarzenberg.

32

33

F.II.
Schauspielhaus.

35

36

37

39

38

40

41 Albertina, weltberühmte Graphik-Sammlung.
42 Österreichisches Museum für angewandte Kunst, am Ring, Säulenhalle.
43 Österreichische Galerie, eine Sammlung österreichischer Kunstwerke des Mittelalters, der Barockzeit, des 19. und 20. Jahrhunderts.
44 Handschriftensammlung der Österreichischen Nationalbibliothek.
45 Die Museen der Stadt Wien mit ihrem Hauptgebäude auf dem Karlsplatz besitzen wichtige Zeugnisse der Wiener Kulturgeschichte.
46 Das Uhrenmuseum gehört zu den Museen der Stadt Wien.
47—52 In der Wiener Innenstadt und in den ehemaligen Vorstädten finden sich immer noch ruhige Plätze und Höfe, die auch wegen ihrer architektonischen und kunsthandwerklichen Details interessant sind.
53 Secession, Ausstellungsgebäude, erbaut von Joseph Maria Olbrich.
54 Postsparkasse, erbaut 1904 von Otto Wagner.
55 Villa Hüttelbergstraße 26, erbaut 1886 von Otto Wagner.
56 Wohnhaus, Linke Wienzeile, erbaut 1898 von Otto Wagner.
57 Kirche Am Steinhof, erbaut 1904—1907 von Otto Wagner.
58 Kärntner Bar, im Kärntner Durchgang, eingerichtet von Adolf Loos.

41 Albertina, the world's most important collection of graphic art.
42 Austrian Museum of Applied Art on the Ring, colonnade.
43 Austrian Gallery, a collection of Austrian art from the Middle Ages, the Baroque period, and the 19th and 20th centuries.
44 Manuscript collection of the Austrian National Library.
45 The Museums of the City of Vienna with their main building on the Karlsplatz possess important testimonies of Viennese cultural history.
46 The Clock Museum is one of the museums of the City of Vienna.
47—52 Many quiet corners and courtyards with details of architectural interest can still be found in the centre and in the former suburbs.
53 Secession. Exhibition hall, built 1897/98 by Joseph Maria Olbrich.
54 Post Office Savings Bank, built 1904 by Otto Wagner.
55 Villa Hüttelbergstraße 26, built 1886 by Otto Wagner.
56 Apartment house, Linke Wienzeile, built 1898 by Otto Wagner.
57 Church of the hospital Am Steinhof, built 1904—1907 by Otto Wagner.
58 Kärntner Bar in the Kärntner passage, designed 1907 by Adolf Loos.

41 Albertina. Collection Graphique de renommée mondiale.
42 Musée Autrichien des Arts Appliqués sur le Ring, salle aux colonnes.
43 Galerie Autrichienne, collection d'oeuvres d'art du Moyen-Age à l'époque baroque et des 19ème et 20ème siècles.
le château du Belvédère.
44 Collection de manuscrits de la Bibliothèque Nationale Autrichienne.
45 Les Musées de la Ville de Vienne avec leur bâtiment principal sur la Karlsplatz, possèdent des oeuvres d'art et des documents de tous genres sur l'histoire culturelle de Vienne.
46 Le Musée des Horloges appartient aux Musées de la Ville de Vienne.
47—52 Dans le centre de la ville de Vienne et dans les anciens faubourgs, on trouve encore des places et des cours tranquilles qui sont intéressantes en raison de leurs détails d'architecture et d'artisanat.
53 Sécession, bâtiment d'exposition, construit en 1897/98 par Joseph Maria Olbrich.
54 Postsparkasse, construite en 1904 par Otto Wagner.
55 Villa, Hüttelbergstraße No 26, construite en 1886 par Otto Wagner.
56 Maison d'habitation, Linke Wienzeile, par Otto Wagner.
57 Eglise de Steinhof, construite de 1904 à 1907 par Otto Wagner.
58 Kärntner Bar, dans le Kärntner Durchgang, décoration intérieure en 1907 par Adolf Loos.

41 Albertina. La raccolta di opere grafiche celebre nel mondo.
42 Museo Austriaco di Arti Applicate sul Ring, sala con colonne.
43 Galleria Austriaca, una collezione di oggetti d'arte austriaca dell'epoca medioevale, barocca e dei secoli XIX e XX.
44 Collezione di manoscritti della Biblioteca Nazionale Austriaca.
45 I Musei della Città di Vienna con il loro edificio principale sulla Karlsplatz sono importanti documenti di storia della cultura di Vienna.
46 Il museo degli orologi fa parte dei Musei della Città di Vienna.
47—52 Nel centro storico di Vienna e negli antichi quartieri periferici si possono scoprire ancora piazze e cortili tranquilli di grande interesse anche per i loro particolari architettonici e artigianali.
53 Secession; palazzo per esposizioni costruito da Joseph Maria Olbrich.
54 Postsparkasse, costruita nel 1904 da Otto Wagner.
55 Villa nella Hüttelbergstraße 26, costruita nel 1886 da Otto Wagner.
56 Abitazione sulla Linke Wienzeile, costruita nel 1898 da Otto Wagner.
57 Chiesa am Steinhof, costruita nel 1904—1907 da Otto Wagner.
58 Kärntner Bar nel Kärntner Durchgang, arredato nel 1907 da Adolf Loos.

41

42

43

45

44

46

47

50

51

48

49

52

53

54

56

55

57

58

An der Stelle der Stadtbefestigungen und des davor gelegenen Glacis wurde in der zweiten Hälfte des 19. Jahrhunderts der die Innenstadt umschließende Straßenzug der Ringstraße angelegt.

59 Akademie der bildenden Künste, erbaut 1872—1876 im Stil der italienischen Renaissance von Theophil Hansen.
60 Justizpalast, erbaut 1875—1881 im Stil der deutschen Renaissance von Alexander Wielemans; Innenhof.
61 Parlament, erbaut 1874—1883 in altgriechischen Stilformen von Theophil Hansen.
62 Universität, erbaut 1873—1874 im Stil der italienischen Renaissance von Heinrich von Ferstel, Arkadengang im Ehrenhof.
63 Votivkirche, erbaut 1856—1879 im Stil der französischen Gotik von Heinrich von Ferstel.
64 Neues Rathaus, erbaut 1872—1883 in gotischem Stil von Friedrich von Schmidt.
65 Ringstraße, Blick auf die Karlskirche.
66 Schloß Belvedere. Prinz Eugen von Savoyen hat es, 150 Jahre vor der Ringstraßenzeit von Lukas von Hildebrandt errichten lassen.

In place of the city fortifications and the surrounding glacis the Ringstraße was built in the second half of the 19th century.

59 Academy of Fine Arts, built 1872—1876 in the Italian Renaissance style by Theophil Hansen.
60 Palace of Justice, built 1875—1881 in the German Renaissance style by Alexander Wielemans; inner courtyard.
61 Parliament, built 1874—1883 following ancient Greek styles by Theophil Hansen.
62 University, built 1873—1874 in the Italien Renaissance style by Heinrich von Ferstel, arcaded Courtyard of Honour.
63 Votive Church, built 1856—1879 in the French Gothic style by Heinrich von Ferstel.
64 New Town Hall, built 1872—1883 in Gothic style by Schmidt.
65 Ringstraße, view towards St. Charles'.
66 Belvedere Palace. Prince Eugene of Savoy had it built by Lukas von Hildebrandt 150 years before the Ringstrassen era.

A l'emplacement des fortifications de la ville et du glacis, on construisit durant la seconde moitié du 19ème siècle l'avenue du Ring qui entoure la ville intérieure.

59 Académie des Beaux Arts, construite de 1872 à 1876 dans le style de la Renaissance italienne par Theophil Hansen.
60 Palais de Justice, construit de 1875 à 1881 dans le style de la Renaissance allemande par Alexander Wielemans; cour intérieure.
61 Parlement, construit de 1874 à 1883 dans l'ancien style grec par Theophil Hansen.
62 Université, construite de 1873 à 1874 dans le style de la Renaissance italienne par Heinrich von Ferstel cour d'honneur à arcades.
63 Votivkirche, construite de 1874 à 1879 dans le style gothique français par Heinrich von Ferstel.
64 Nouvel Hôtel de Ville, construit de 1872 à 1883 dans le style gothique par Friedrich von Schmidt.
65 Avenue du Ring, vue sur l'église Saint-Charles.
66 Château du Belvédère. Le prince Eugène de Savoie le fit construire par Lukas von Hildebrandt 150 ans avant l'époque du Ring.

Al posto delle fortificazioni della città e del Glacis che si apriva di fronte ad esse, fu realizzato il tracciato della Ringstraße (seconda metà del secolo XIX) attorno alla città interna.

59 Accademia delle Belle Arti, costruita nel 1872—1876 su progetto di Theophil Hansen nello stile del rinascimento italiano.
60 Palazzo di Giustizia, costruito nel 1875—1881 da Alexander Wielemans nello stile del rinascimento tedesco; cortile interno.
61 Parlamento, costruito nel 1874—1883 da Theophil Hansen nello stile greco antico.
62 Università, costruita nel 1873—1874 da Heinrich von Ferstel nello stile del rinascimento italiano arcata del cortile d'onore.
63 Votivkirche (Chiesa Votiva), costruita nel 1856—1879 da Heinrich von Ferstel nello stile gotico francese.
64 Neues Rathaus (nuovo Municipio), costruito nel 1872—1883 da Friedrich von Schmidt nello stile gotico.
65 Ringstraße, vista sulla chiesa di San Carlo.
66 Castello Belvedere. Della sua costruzione fu incaricato Lukas von Hildebrandt dal principe Eugenio di Savoia 150 anni prima dell'epoca della Ringstraße.

59

60

62

64

Mobil

Schloß Schönbrunn sollte zuerst auf der Anhöhe stehen, wo heute die Gloriette steht. Erst der zweite Entwurf Johann Bernhard Fischers von Erlach wurde ausgeführt. Der Bau wurde 1695 begonnen und, mit verschiedenen Umbauten, unter Maria Theresia 1744—1749 beendet.

67 Einer der Schauräume.
68 Schönbrunner Schloßtheater.
69 Palmenhaus.
70 Wagenburg.
71 Motiv aus dem Schönbrunner Schloßpark.
72 Gesamtansicht des Schlosses Schönbrunn von der Gloriette aus.

Schönbrunn Palace was originally planned to look down from the hill where the Gloriette stands today, but it was Johann Bernhard Fischer von Erlach's second design that was carried out. Construction began in 1695 and was finished with various changes and adaptations under Maria Theresia 1744—1749.

67 One of the ceremonial rooms.
68 Schönbrunn Palace Theatre.
69 Palm house.
70 Coach house.
71 Motiv from the Palace Garden.
72 View of Schönbrunn Palace from the Gloriette.

Le château de Schönbrunn aurait dû être à l'origine construit sur la colline où se trouve de nos jours la Gloriette. Ce n'est que le second projet de Johann Fischer von Erlach que l'on réalisa. La construction fut commencée en 1695 et terminée sous Marie-Thérèse de 1744 à 1749 après de nombreuses modifications.

67 Une des salles.
68 Théâtre du château de Schönbrunn.
69 Palmeraie.
70 Musée des voitures.
71 Motif du parc du château de Schönbrunn.
72 Vue totale du château de Schönbrunn à partir de la Gloriette.

Il castello Schönbrunn avrebbe dovuto sorgere sull'altura sulla quale oggi c'è la Gloriette. La sua costruzione fu eseguita su un secondo progetto di Johann Bernhard Fischer von Erlach. La sua esecuzione iniziò nel 1695 e, dopo numerose trasfomazioni, fu completata nel 1744—1749 sotto Maria Teresa.

67 Una delle sale.
68 Teatro del castello Schönbrunn.
69 Serra di palme.
70 Rimessa per le carrozze.
71 Particolare del parco del castello Schönbrunn.
72 Veduta d'insieme del castello Schönbrunn dalla Gloriette.

67

68

71

„Vor der Stadt“ liegen nicht nur die Schlösser Belvedere und Schönbrunn mit ihren Sammlungen, sondern auch das von Karl Schwanzer 1958 geschaffene Museum des 20. Jahrhunderts, das Heeresgeschichtliche Museum im Arsenal und, im Westen, das Technische Museum.

73 Museum des 20. Jahrhunderts, Aktion.
74 Heeresgeschichtliches Museum, Feldschlangen.
75 Technisches Museum.

Beliebte Wiener Institutionen haben meist eine alte Tradition — mitunter aber gewinnen sie ihre Beliebtheit schon kurz nach ihrer Einführung, weil sie dem Wesen dieser Stadt und ihrer Bewohner entsprechen. Dazu gehören alle Straßen und Plätze, die verkehrsfrei gemacht werden und so zum beschaulichen Schlendern, zum Schauen und zum Einkaufen verlocken.

76 Konditorei Demel auf dem Kohlmarkt.
77 Versteigerung im Dorotheum.

Not only the Palaces of Belvedere and Schönbrunn with their collections lie “outside the city”, but also the Museum of the Twentieth Century designed by Karl Schwanzer in 1958, the Military History Museum in the Arsenal and the Museum of Technology.

73 Museum of the Twentieth Century, happening.
74 Museum of Military History, late Medieval field piece.
75 Museum of Technology.

Popular Viennese institutions usually have an ancient tradition—just occasionally, however, there is such a thing as instant popularity because an innovation corresponds to the character of the city and its inhabitants. That was the case with all the roads and squares from which cars have been banned and which are now taken over by people strolling, looking, and shopping.

76 Konditorei Demel on the Kohlmarkt.
77 Auction in the Dorotheum.

«Devant la ville» se trouvent non seulement les châteaux du Belvédère et de Schönbrunn avec leurs collections mais aussi le Musée du 20ème siècle fondé par Karl Schwanzer en 1958, le Musée Historique de l'Armée dans l'Arsenal et à l'Ouest le Musée Technique.

73 Musée du 20ème siècle, manifestation.
74 Musée Historique de l'Armée, canon.
75 Musée Technique.

Des institutions chères aux Viennois ont la plupart une tradition ancienne, elles gagnent surtout leur popularité peu de temps après leur création, car elles correspondent au caractère de la ville et de ses habitants. Il faut citer toutes les rues et les places d'où l'on a banni la circulation automobile et qui incitent à la flânerie, à regarder et à acheter.

76 Confiserie Demel sur le Kohlmarkt.
77 Vente aux enchères au Dorotheum.

„Vor der Stadt“ («fuori delle antiche mura cittadine») si possono ammirare non solo il castello Belvedere e Schönbrunn, ma anche il museo del XX secolo, opera di Karl Schwanzer (1958), il museo di storia militare nell'Arsenale e, più ad ovest, il museo della tecnica.

73 Museo del XX secolo, manifestazione.
74 Museo di storia militare, colubrine.
75 Museo della tecnica.

Popolari istituzioni viennesi hanno per la maggior parte un'antica tradizione. Non di rado la loro popolarità nasce quasi parallelamente alla loro creazione, esse infatti sono espressione dello spirito di questa città e dei suoi abitanti. Ne sono un esempio le strade e le piazze dove il traffico automobilistico viene a poco a poco eliminato e che sono diventate il luogo preferito per piacevoli passeggiate, distrazioni, acquisti.

76 Pasticceria Demel nel Kohlmarkt.
77 Asta nel Dorotheum.

73

74

PETRAVIC
DAMPFTURBINE

78 Schönlaterngasse: mehrere Galerien, Restaurants, die Alte Schmiede mit dem Libresso, den Ausstellungsräumen, dem Vortragssaal und dem originellen Kellerlokal.
79 Altstadtensemble vor der Kirche Maria am Gestade: ein ruhiger Platz mitten in der Stadt.
80 Kohlmarkt, Fußgängerzone.
81 Augarten-Porzellan, Blick in die Verkaufsstelle. Das Wiener Kunsthandwerk bietet außer diesem Porzellan mit dem Bindenschild wertvolle Goldschmiedearbeiten, Emailarbeiten, Puppen, Keramik und kostbare Glaswaren.
82 Wiener Glaswaren, Verkaufsstelle in der Kärntnerstraße.
83 Hotel Sacher, traditionsreich und legendenreich; die nach Geheimrezepten hergestellte Sacher-Torte wird in alle Welt versandt.
84 Zwölfapostelkeller, Stadtkeller in der Sonnenfelsgasse.
85 Fußgängerzone Kärntnerstraße: die traditionelle Wiener Einkaufsstraße.

78 Schönlaterngasse: several galleries, restaurants, the Alte Schmiede (old smithy) with its libresso, exhibition rooms, lecture hall and the tavern in the vaults.
79 Old town ensemble in front of the church Maria am Gestade: a quiet corner in the middle of the city.
80 Kohlmarkt, pedestrian zone.
81 Augarten china, view of the shop. Beside this fine china with the crowned shield mark, Viennese crafts include valuable goldsmiths' works, enamel, dolls, ceramics, pottery and precious glass.
82 Viennese glass ware. Shop in Kärntnerstraße.
83 Hotel Sacher, rich in tradition and surrounded by legend. The Sacher cake, with its jealously guarded secret recipe, is sent to all corners of the world.
84 Zwölfapostelkeller (twelve disciples' cellar), city vault in Sonnenfelsgasse.
85 Kärntnerstraße pedestrian zone: the traditional shopping street of the Viennese.

78 Schönlaterngasse: nombreuses galeries, restaurants, la Vieille Forge avec le «libresso», les salles d'exposition, la salle de conférences et la cave très originale.
79 Quartier de la vieille ville devant l'église Maria am Gestade: place tranquille au centre de la ville.
80 Kohlmarkt, zone pour piétons.
81 Porcelaine de Augarten, vue du magasin. L'artisanat viennois présente en plus de cette porcelaine de précieux travaux de joaillerie, des travaux d'émaux, des poupées, de la céramique et de la verrerie.
82 Verrerie viennoise, point de vente dans la Kärntnerstraße.
83 Hôtel Sacher, riche en traditions et légendes. La tarte Sacher dont la recette est un secret de la maison est envoyée dans le monde entier.
84 Cave des Douze Apôtres, cave de la ville dans la Sonnenfelsgasse.
85 Zone piétonnière de la Kärntnerstraße: la traditionelle rue commerçante de Vienne.

78 Schönlaterngasse: numerose gallerie, ristoranti, la Alte Schmiede (vecchia forgia) con il Libresso (caffè dei letterati), i locali per le esposizioni, la sala per le conferenze e con il caffè sotterraneo.
79 Gruppo di antiche costruzioni di fronte alla chiesa Maria am Gestade: un angolo tranquillo nel centro della città.
80 Kohlmarkt, zona pedonale.
81 Porcellana di Augarten, vista del locale di vendita. L'artigianato viennese offre oltre a questo genere di porcellane con motivi floreali, preziosi articoli di oreficeria, lavori in smalto, bambole, ceramiche e preziosi lavori in vetro.
82 Lavori in vetro viennesi, locale di vendita nella Kärntnerstraße.
83 Hotel Sacher, tradizionale e leggendario; la «torta Sacher», un dolce creato secondo una ricetta segreta, è diffuso in tutto il mondo.
84 Zwölfapostelkeller (cantina dei dodici Apostoli), cantina cittadina nella Sonnenfelsgasse.
85 Zona pedonale nella Kärntnerstraße: la tradizionale strada commerciale di Vienna.

78

79

FRANCISCVS IOSEPHVS I
PERFECIT A D MDCCCXCIII
APOTHEKE
ORDEN
Rothe
PARFUMERIE
B&S
House of Gentlemen
WIEN I.
Rodenstock Optik
INTER
HALTEN VERBOTEN
Anfang
Ende

81

82

83

84

METRO
City
CAFE BAR
ELBEO
Strümpfe
ITTNER
benger
NACH UNGARN
MIT IBUSZ
NORDSTERN
WIENER
SPAR- u. KREDIT-
INSTITUT
W. GERSTENBERGER
RESTAURANT
RESTAURANT
AMBASSADOR
All rooms
air conditioned
HOTEL AMBASSADOR

45

Bilder als Hinweise für eine Stadtbesichtigung:

86 Stadtpark, Kursalon. Der Stadtpark wurde nach der Schleifung der Stadtbefestigungen auf der Fläche des „Wasserglacis" als Park in englischem Stil angelegt.
87 Johann-Strauß-Denkmal, eines der vielen Denkmäler des Stadtparks.
88 Eislaufverein und Konzerthaus.
89 Teil aus dem architektonischen Abschluß der Wienfluß-Einwölbung im Stadtpark; Entwurf von Friedrich Ohmann, 1903.
90 Beethoven-Haus in der Probusgasse. Hier entstand das „Heiligenstädter Testament".
91 „Figarohaus", Schulerstraße 8, Mozarts Sterbehaus. Es enthält Gedenkräume, die von den Museen der Stadt Wien eingerichtet sind.
92 Barockmuseum im Unteren Belvedere, die Original-Bleifiguren des 1737—1739 von Georg Raphael Donner für den Neuen Markt geschaffenen Providentiabrunnens.
93 Palais Schwarzenberg, Marmorsaal.

Suggestions for a walk round the city:

86 Stadtpark, pumphouse. The city park was laid out on the area of the former "Wasserglacis" after the razing of the city fortifications, on the model of an English garden.
87 Johann-Strauß-Memorial, one of the many sculptures in the Stadtpark.
88 Ice rink and Konzerthaus.
89 Part of the architectural head to the Wienfluß tunnel in the Stadtpark; design by Friedrich Ohmann, 1903.
90 Beethoven-house in Probusgasse. The "Heiligenstädter Testament" was written here.
91 Figaro house, Schulerstraße 8, the house where Mozart died. It contains memorial rooms furnished by the Museums of the City of Vienna.
92 Baroque Museum in the Lower Belvedere, the original lead sculptures created by Georg Raphael Donner 1737—1739 for the Providentia Fountain on the Neuer Markt.
93 Palais Schwarzenberg, marble gallery.

Photos de curiosités conseillées lors d'une visite de la ville:

86 Stadtpark. Kursalon. Le Stadtpark fut tracé après la démolition des fortifications de la ville à l'emplacement du «glacis d'eau» dans le style des parc anglais.
87 Monument de Johann Strauß, un des nombreux monuments du Stadtpark.
88 Association sportive de patinage et Konzerthaus.
89 Partie du fronton du tunnel de la Vienne dans le Stadtpark; projet de Friedrich Ohmann, 1903.
90 Maison de Beethoven dans la Probusgasse. Ici fut écrit le «Testament de Heiligenstadt».
91 «Maison de Figaro», Schulerstraße No 8, maison mortuaire de Mozart, Elle renferme des salles du souvenir qui sont aménagées par les Musées de la Ville de Vienne.
92 Musée Baroque dans le Belvédère Inférieur. Figures de plomb réalisées de 1737 à 1739 par Georg Raphael Donner pour la fontaine de la Providence sur le Neuer Markt.
93 Palais Schwarzenberg, galerie de marbre.

Illustrazioni-guida per una vista della città:

86 Stadtpark, Kursalon. Lo Stadtpark (Parco civico) è sorto sull'area che aveva il nome di «Wasserglacis» dopo la demolazione dei bastioni della città; è stato tracciato in stile inglese.
87 Monumento a Johann Strauß, uno dei numerosi monumenti nel parco civico.
88 Associazione di pattinaggio e Konzerthaus.
89 Particolare dello sbocco architettonico della copertura a volta del fiume Wien nel parco civico; progetto di Friedrich Ohmann, 1903.
90 Casa di Beethoven nella Probusgasse. Qui egli compose lo «Heiligenstädter Testament».
91 «Figarohaus» (casa di Figaro), casa di morte di Mozart. È stato dichiarato monumento nazionale ed è possibile visitare le sue stanze che sono affidate alle cure dei Musei della Città di Vienna.
92 Museo barocco nel Belvedere inferiore; statue di piombo originali del 1737—1739 di Georg Raphael Donner, create per la Providentiabrunnen (fontana della Providenza) nella piazza Neuer Markt.
93 Pailais Schwarzenberg, sala di marmo.

86

87

8

89

0

91

3

Bilder als Hinweise für eine Stadtbesichtigung:

94 Maria-Theresien-Denkmal, zwischen den beiden Museen auf dem Ring, ein Werk von Kaspar von Zumbusch, 1888 enthüllt:
95 Kapuzinergruft auf dem Neuen Markt, Begräbnisstätte der Habsburger.
96 Platz Am Hof mit dem Collaltopalais, alten Bürgerhäusern und dem Bürgerlichen Zeughaus. Hier befand sich von der Mitte des 12. Jahrhunderts an die Residenz der Babenberger.
97 Pestsäule am Graben, gestiftet im Pestjahr 1679 von Kaiser Leopold I., geweiht 1693, ein Werk, an dem Matthias Rauchmiller, Fischer von Erlach der Ältere, Lodovico Burnacini und Paul Strudel beteiligt sind.
98—106 Wiener Milieu — für nostalgische Naturen. Mit diesen Bildern ist zwar Typisches erfaßt, sie zeigen aber nur eine Facette des vielfältigen Bildes dieser Stadt.

Suggestions for a walk round the city:

94 Maria Theresia Memorial between the two Museums on the Ring, by Kaspar von Zumbusch, unveiled 1888.
95 Capucchin vault on Neuer Markt, burial place of the Hapsburgs.
96 Square Am Hof with the Collalto palace, old burghers' houses and the Citizens' Armory. This was the site of the Babenberg residence in the middle of the twelfth century.
97 Plague column on the Graben, dedicated by Emperor Leopold I in the plague year 1679, consecrated in 1693, a joint work by Matthias Rauchmiller, Fischer von Erlach the Elder, Lodovico Burnacini and Paul Strudel.
98—106 Viennese milieus—for nostalgic natures. These pictures do indeed show typical facets, but only facets of the varied image of this city.

Photos de curiosités conseillées lors d'une visite de la ville:

94 Monument de Marie-Thérèse, entre les deux musées sur le Ring, oeuvre de Kaspar von Zumbusch, inauguré en 1888.
95 Crypte des Capucins sur le Neuer Markt, cercueils de la famille des Habsbourg.
96 Place Am Hof avec le palais Collalto, vieilles maisons bourgeoises et l'Arsenal bourgeois. C'est ici que se trouvait à partir de la moitié du 12ème siècle la résidence des Babenberg.
97 Colonne de la Peste sur le Graben, don de l'empereur Léopold I en 1679, année de l'épidémie de peste, consacrée en 1693, oeuvre à laquelle ont participé Matthias Rauchmiller, Fischer von Erlach-père, Lodovico Burnacini et Paul Strudel.
98—106 Milieu viennois — pour les naturels nostalgiques. Ces photos illustrent un aspect typique mais ne montrent qu'une des facettes du caractère très varié de cette ville.

Immagini-guida per una visita della città:

94 Monumento a Maria Teresa tra i due musei sul Ring, opera di Kaspar von Zumbusch, scoperto nel 1888:
95 Kapuzinergruft (Cripta dei Cappuccini) nella piazza Neuer Markt, tomba degli Asburgo.
96 Piazza Am Hof con il palazzo Collalto, antiche case borghesi e arsenale civico. Qui si trovava la residenza dei Babenberger dalla metà del secolo XII in poi.
97 Colonna della peste nel Graben, promessa in voto dall'imperatore Leopoldo I durante l'epidemia della peste dell'anno 1679, consacrata nel 1693, opera di Matthias Rauchmiller, Fischer von Erlach il vecchio, Lodovico Burnacini e Paul Strudel.
98—106 Ambiente viennese — per nature nostalgiche. Queste illustrazioni costituiscono soltanto un esempio tipico degli svariati aspetti di questa città.

94

95

98

99

100

101

102

103

104

105

106

107 Andromedabrunnen, im Hof des Alten Rathauses, 1741 von Georg Raphael Donner geschaffen.
108 Brunnen im Savoyischen Damenstift, Johannesgasse 15—17, 1766—1770 von Johann Martin Fischer geschaffen.
109 Biedermeierhaus aus dem Jahr 1803, Schreyvogelgasse 10.
110—115 Gut essen, gut trinken, sich gut unterhalten — berechtigte Wünsche von Menschen, die hart arbeiten, in Wien so wie überall.
116—121 Wiener Prater: Seit der Freigabe des kaiserlichen Jagdgebietes in den Donauauen für die Öffentlichkeit durch Joseph II., 1766, ist er der beliebteste Erholungs- und Belustigungsort der Wiener.

107 Andromeda fountain in the courtyard of the Old Town Hall, created 1741 by Georg Raphael Donner.
108 Fountain in the Savoy' Foundation for Ladies, Johannesgasse 15—17, created by Johann Martin Fischer, 1766—1770.
109 Biedermeier house from the year 1803, Schreyvogelgasse 10.
110—115 Eat well, drink well, have fun—hard-working peoples' well-earnt desires, in Vienna and anywhere else.
116—121 Vienna Prater: Since Joseph II opened the Imperial hunting grounds in the Danube riparian region to the public in 1766, the Prater has been the favourite place of recreation and amusement for the Viennese.

107 Fontaine d'Andromède, dans la cour de l'ancien Hôtel de Ville, réalisée en 1741 par Georg Raphael Donner.
108 Fontaine dans le Savoyischer Damenstift, Johannesgasse No 15—17, réalisée de 1766 à 1770 par Johann Martin Fischer.
109 Maison Biedermeier de l'année 1803, Schreyvogelgasse No 10.
110—115 Bien manger, bien boire, bien s'amuser, souhait compréhensible des hommes qui travaillent beaucoup à Vienne comme partout ailleurs.
116—121 Prater viennois: depuis l'ouverture au public par Joseph II du domaine de chasse impérial sur les rives du Danube en 1766, il est devenu le lieu de détente et d'amusement préféré des Viennois.

107 Fontana di Andromeda, nel cortile dell'antico Municipio, ideata nel 1741 da Georg Raphael Donner.
108 Fontana nell'Ospizio Femminile Savoiardo, Johannesgasse 15—17, ideata nel 1766—1770 da Johann Martin Fischer.
109 Casa Biedermeier al numero 10 della Schreyvogelgasse.
110—115 Mangiare e bere bene, conversare piacevolmente — giusti desideri di tutti coloro che lavorano molto, a Vienna come dovunque.
116—121 Il Prater di Vienna: nel 1776, in seguito all'apertura al pubblico della riserva di caccia imperiale nelle praterie lungo il Danubio ad opera di Giuseppe II, esso rappresenta il luogo di ricreazione e di divertimento più amato dai Viennesi.

107

108

10

110

113

114

111

112

115

116

117

119

118

120

121

122 Flohmarkt auf dem Platz Am Hof.
123 Mariahilfer Straße zur Weihnachtszeit.
124 Kirtagsstand.

Viele Wiener Institutionen und Bauwerke der Vergangenheit, die das geistige und optische Stadtbild mitbestimmen, werden heute von der Verwaltung der Stadt gefördert und erhalten. Die Stadt Wien initiiert und verwirklicht aber auch in der Gegenwart ein großes Programm städtebaulicher, kultureller und sozialer Projekte.

125—129 Wohnhausanlagen der Stadt Wien, „Gemeindebauten", aus der Zeit der Ersten Republik, 1918—1934. Die architektonisch bedeutendste Anlage dieser Zeit ist der Karl-Marx-Hof (128).

130—135 Neben den Wohnbauten der Stadt Wien sind in der Gegenwart die sozialen Einrichtungen von besonderer Bedeutung: Schulen, Kindergärten, Krankenhäuser, Kindertagesheime, Einkaufszentren, Studentenheime, Verkehrsanlagen, Parks, Sportanlagen.

122 Flea market on the square Am Hof.
123 Mariahilfer Straße at Christmas time.
124 Stall at the festival of a local church's patron saint. Many Viennese institutions and buildings from the past which determine the spiritual and visual image of the city, are now supported and maintained by the city administration. The city of Vienna also initiates and realizes a generous programme of urban planning as well as cultural and social projects.

125—129 Housing estates of the City of Vienna from the time of the First Republic, 1918—1934. The most important architectural achievement of that time is Karl-Marx-Hof (128).

130—135 Apart from municipal housing, social institutions are of particular importance today: schools, kindergartens, hospitals, day schools, shopping centres, students' hostels, traffic buildings, parks, sports-grounds.

122 Marché aux puces sur la place Am Hof.
123 Mariahilfer Straße à la période de Noël.
124 Stand de foire.

De nombreuses institutions viennoises et bâtiments du passé qui déterminent le caractère et l'aspect de la ville sont actuellement subventionnés et entretenus par l'Administration de la Ville. Mais la Ville de Vienne projette et réalise également de nos jours un grand programme de réalisations urbaines, culturelles et sociales.

125—129 Cités d'habitation de la Ville de Vienne, «cités communales» de l'époque de la 1ère République, 1918—1934. Le complexe le plus important au point de vue architectonique et datant de cette époque est la cité Karl Marx (128).

130—135 En plus des immeubles d'habitation de la Ville de Vienne, les institutions sociales récentes sont d'une grande importance: écoles, jardins d'enfants, hôpitaux, centres d'accueil pour enfants, centres commerciaux, foyers d'étudiants, moyens de transport, parcs, terrains de sport.

122 Il mercato delle pulci nella piazza Am Hof.
123 La Mariahilfer Straße nel periodo natalizio.
124 Chiosco di vendita in occasione della Giornata della Chiesa.

Molte istituzioni ed edifici viennesi che appartengono al passato e che caratterizzano l'immigine ottica e spirituale della città, sono oggi affidati alle cure e alla manutenzione dell'amministrazione civica. La Città di Vienna ha iniziato e realizza anche oggi un imponente programma di opere edilizie, culturali e sociali.

125—129 Quartieri d'abitazione della Città di Vienna «Edifici dell'ammistrazione comunale» dell'epoca della prima Repubblica, 1914—1934. Il più importante complesso architettonico di quel periodo è il Karl-Marx-Hof (128).

130—135 Oltre alle case d'abitazione della Città di Vienna, sono oggi degne di essere menzionate altre importanti opere nel settore dell'edilizia sociale: scuole, asili infantili, ospedali, giardini d'infanzia, centri commerciali, case dello studente, reti stradali, parchi, centri sportivi.

122

123

24

125

126

128

127

129

130

133

134

131

132

135

136, 137 Wiener Stadthalle, eine Mehrzweckanlage für kulturelle, religiöse und sportliche Veranstaltungen. Erbaut 1953—1958 von Roland Rainer.
138 Blick auf die Wiener Internationale Gartenschau (WIG) 1964.
139 Blick auf das Gebäude der WIG 1974.
140 Leopoldsberg, Wander- und Erholungsgebiet, Hausberg der Wiener.
141 Flußlandschaft der Lobau im Süden der Stadt mit ihrem tiefsten Punkt, 151 m ü. d. M.
142 U-Bahn-Tunnel.
143 Blick aus der U-Bahn-Baustelle auf dem Stephansplatz.
144 Neue Wohnviertel im Nordosten der Stadt. Großfeldsiedlung.
145 Die Donau erhält bei Wien ein zweites Gerinne. So entsteht eine langgestreckte Donauinsel mit einem neuen Erholungsgebiet für die Wiener, es wird absoluter Hochwasserschutz erreicht, und der Grundwasserspiegel wird in weitem Umkreis ansteigen.
146 Internationales Amtssitz- und Konferenzzentrum Wien, „Uno-City".

136, 137 Vienna City Hall, a multi-purpose centre for cultural, religious and sporting events. Built 1953—1958 by Roland Rainer.
138 View of the Vienna International Horticultural Exhibition (WIG) 1964 building from the Danube tower.
139 View of the WIG 1974 building.
140 Leopoldsberg, a region for walking and recreation, the "home hill" of the Viennese.
141 Riparian landscape of the Lobau in the South of the city, its lowest point is 151 m above sea level.
142 Subway tunnel.
143 View from the subway building site on Stephansplatz.
144 New housing estates North-East of the city. Großfeldsiedlung.
145 The Danube will receive a second bed near Vienna, which will provide a long Danube island with a new recreation area for the Viennese, secure absolute flood protection and raise the groundwater level within a wide radius.
146 International office and conference centre Vienna, „UNO-City".

136—137 Palais des Sports, bâtiment qui peut être utilisé pour des manifestations culturelles, religieuses et sportives, construit de 1953 à 1958 par Roland Rainer.
138 Vue sur le bâtiment de l'Exposition Internationale d'Horticulture de Vienne (WIG) en 1964, depuis la tour du Danube.
139 Vue sur le bâtiment de la WIG 1974.
140 Leopoldsberg, lieu d'excursion et de détente, «montagne» des Viennois.
141 Site fluvial de la Lobau au Sud de Vienne, point le plus bas de la ville (alt. 151 m).
142 Tunnel du Métro.
143 Vue prise à partir d'un chantier du métro sur la place Saint-Etienne.
144 Nouveau quartier d'habitation au Nord-Est de la ville. Cité de Großfeld.
145 Le Danube a dans Vienne un second canal d'écoulement. Il en résulte une longue île sur le Danube avec un nouveau centre de détente. Elle sera absolument protégée des innondations. Le niveau de la nappe aquifère en sera relevé dans un vaste périmètre.
146 Centre de conférences et siège d'organisations internationales, UNO-City, sur la rive gauche du Danube.

136 e 137 La Stadthalle di Vienna, un vasto centro per manifestazioni culturali, religiose e sportive. Costruito da Roland Rainer nel 1953—1958.
138 Vista del palazzo dell'Esposizione Internazionale di Giardinaggio di Vienna (WIG, 1964) dalla torre del Danubio.
139 Vista del palazzo della WIG, 1974.
140 Leopoldsberg, meta di passeggiate e di ristoro; la collina preferita dai Viennesi.
141 Paesaggio fluviale della Lobau a sud della città; il punto più basso: 151 metri sopra il livello del mare.
142 Galleria della metropolitana.
143 Vista dal cantiere della metropolitana sulla piazza di Santo Stefano.
144 Nuovo quartiere d'abitazione a nord-est della città. Centro abitato di Großfeld.
145 Un secondo corso d'acqua si dirama dal Danubio; si forma così una lunga isola che è meta di ristoro per i Viennesi, si crea un elemento protettivo contro le piene e la possibilità di aumento del livello dell'acqua si estende in questo modo ad un raggio molto più vasto.
146 La sede di organizzazioni e congressi internazionali di Vienna, la «UNO-City» sulla riva sinistra del Danubio.

136

137

138

139

140

141

142

144

143

145

46

147 Bau einer Wohnungsgenossenschaft, Inzersdorfer Straße.
148 Stadt des Kindes, ein Heim für rund 260 meist milieugeschädigte Kinder, das nach neuen architektonischen und erzieherischen Konzepten errichtet wurde und geführt wird.
149 Praterbrücke.
150 Wienerwald. Ihm verdanken die Wiener vor allem, daß sie noch immer eine bessere Luft in ihrer Stadt haben, als das in anderen Großstädten der Welt der Fall ist.

147 Apartment house of a housing co-operative, Inzersdorfer Straße.
148 Children's City, a home for about 260 children, most of them from problem backgrounds, designed and administered to new architectural and educational concepts.
149 Prater bridge.
150 Vienna Woods. Thanks to the Vienna Woods, the Viennese still enjoy better air than other city-dwellers.

147 Construction d'une cité d'habitation, Inzersdorfer Straße.
148 Ville de l'Enfant, maison d'enfant prévue pour 260 enfants provenant de familles inaptes à leur éducation, conçue et dirigée d'après de nouveaux concepts architectoniques et éducatifs.
149 Pont du Prater.
150 Forêt viennoise. C'est à elle que les Viennois doivent avant tout le «bon air» de leur ville. Il est meilleur que dans les autres grandes villes du monde.

147 Costruzione di una società edilizia, Inzersdorfer Straße.
148 Città del Bambino, una casa d'assistenza all'infanzia per circa 260 bambini in gran parte vittime di condizioni sociali sfavorevoli; è costruito secondo concetti architettonici moderni e basato su nuove concezioni pedagogiche.
149 Ponte del Prater.
150 Foresta Viennese. Rende l'aria della città di Vienna migliore che in molte altre grandi città.

147

148

49